It's

All

Good!

Daily Affirmations for Teens

Teresa Ann Willis

Jazz

Thank you
for your support
and your love. And
thanks for sharing

Peace and Blessings

Love

Teresa

Emp!Emp! Press
Washington, DC

Library of Congress Catalog Card Number

96-85676

ISBN 0-9667677-0-5

Acknowledgments

I have so many people to thank for helping me as I wrote this book. Those who helped me out financially, friends who did Nexis searches for me, family and friends who offered encouragement and insight, people who inspired me and didn't even know it, and lastly, all the kids who shared their triumphs, their tragedies, their truths with me. Thank You!

Thanks Darlene and Joe, Marie and Lofton (aka Mom and Dad), Aunt Mae, Michael Craig Alexander, Michelle Fuller, James Shivers, Tom Henry, Dr. Aline Smith, Lisa Richardson, Adrienne Johnson, Sonya Beard, Greg Dickerson, Umar Lambright, Greg Morrison, Bobby Jackson, Mark Will-Weber, Janice Stone, Laurie Denise Willis, Aaron Willis, Janice Walker Willis, Susan L. Taylor, Farai Chideya, Marianne Rivera, Dennis Kelly, Susan Ravitz, Gwendolyn Allen, Francis Minnis, Lucas Rivera, Pat and Mr. Hartman, Chuck Payne, Sylvia Chambers, Robert Willis, Chris Heredia, Patty Jackson, WDAS FM, Damon Williams, Christina Head, Nikki Matos, Iyanla Vanzant, Gary Zukav, Mr. King, Steve Payano, Donna Debus-Hawk, Alicia I.R. DeNardo, Pat Ross, Dean Young, Norma Shriver,

Vicki Sellitto, Neeti Madan, Karen Marnell, Mahmoudah, Malik Yoba, Jackie Threadgill, Kim Collins, Linda Cameron, all the librarians at the Allentown and Bethlehem libraries, all the kids in juvy—Tyreek, Eggy, Wanda, Wendy, Corey and the entire crew, all the kids who gave interviews and their input for the book, Chandra Sparks—my wonderful editor—Donald Wayne Blount who gave his love and support and also contributed a page in this book, and Theta R. Pavis-Weil who sat on my front porch and told me not to give up. I didn't!

Permissions

Thanks to all those who granted me permission to use their words to help reach the young folks!

And ten gazillion thanks to all those quoted for their words of encouragement, wisdom and insight.

This book is dedicated to

Matthew "Magic Matt" Willis
who contributed a page in this book before
moving on

Irma Best-Williams and **Aline Smith**
who helped me get through

and

Robert "Yummy" Sandifer and **Eric Norah**
who inspired me to write this book

Word!

Teenagers, finally, a daily affirmation book written just for you! As teens, you're in the early and middle stages of the growth and maturation process. Your hormones have begun flipping, you're undergoing physical changes and you alternate between feeling good about yourselves, your parents and your future and hating everything and everybody, parents included! It's a confusing time for you.

It's All Good! will help you get through these difficult times by giving you encouragement, insight and hope about your lives and your future.

It's All Good! is for those of you who think you can and those of you who aren't so sure! It's for those who think you know all the answers and those who have so many questions. It's for those who are struggling with life and those who need that extra little push to get going.

It's All Good! is divided into three sections. The first section deals with self-esteem, fear, peer pressure, drugs, violence, hope, friends, school, partying, God and spirituality, racism, love, hate, giving up and not giving up, teen self-image, winning and losing, respect and disrespect, forgiveness, learning disabilities, The Golden Rule and the future.

In this section, you'll learn how to tackle the challenges you face at home and in school with classmates, coaches and teachers and you'll learn how to deal with the challenges lurking in the streets.

The second section looks at racism, racial stereotypes, being bi or multiracial, skin color prejudice and the whole idea of "race" in America. This section also includes African-American, Euro-American, Asian-American, Latino and Native American history.

The third section deals with sex and relationships and everything related to sex and relationships for teens. There's information on boys respecting girls, girls respecting boys, sexually transmitted diseases, teen dating violence, teens who injure themselves, eating disorders and more. Additionally, this section offers helpful advice on how to better handle the difficult task of being teen parents.

In all sections and on each day, there is a phrase or *affirmation,* you can memorize. By repeating the affirmation—either silently or aloud or, by writing it down, you will begin to think and act differently.

If you're in the habit of saying prayers at night or praying whenever you feel the need, you can include the affirmations in your prayers.

Or, you can simply say or write the affirmations several times throughout the day. And whenever things start to get a little rough, instead of repeating negative statements and thinking negative thoughts, repeat one of your affirmations and *be* positive!!!

I am proud of you for picking up this book and reading it each day. Doing something over and over teaches you discipline. And discipline is one of the things that will help you reach your goals. I have faith in you, and I know you *can* and *will* reach your goals and your highest potential!

Peace

When I look in the mirror I see . . .

January 1

My mother is my root, my foundation. She planted the seed that I base my life on and that is the belief that the ability to achieve starts in your mind.
—Michael Jordan

No one else can make you feel good about who you are unless, deep down, you feel good about who you are. And unless you believe in your ability to achieve and become successful—you never will. During his sophomore year, Michael Jordan got cut from his high school basketball team. He grew several inches, tried out again his junior and made the team. Michael didn't give up because his mother encouraged him to keep trying, and because he knew what he could do even when the coach didn't. You've got to know what you can do. You've got to believe in yourself and in your ability to achieve great things, even if no one else does.

I believe in myself! I am good enough!

January 2

Even in our fractured state, all of us count and fit somewhere.
—Jesse Jackson

It's normal for you not to like many things about yourself. When your parents were 14, they had pimples too. Some of them were sent to the principal's office just like some of you have been. The problem for too many kids is that your self-esteem is wack! Self-esteem is what you believe about your worth in the world and what you believe about your ability to accomplish the things you want to accomplish. Repeating your affirmations will help you to believe good things about yourself. Still, beliefs don't change overnight. But they *can* change if you want them to. If you believe you're dumb, you'll act dumb even though you really are smart. If you believe you're a bad kid, you'll act like a bad kid. Choosing to do good is just as easy as choosing to do bad. But first, you have to believe in your goodness.

I believe in myself. I am a good person.

January 3

I didn't have high self-esteem when I was a teenager, as I think most teenagers don't.
—Alanis Morissette

How do you feel about yourself? If you're not feeling too good these days, why? The only way you're ever going to have high self-esteem is to understand just how special you are. What do you mean "no, I'm not!" You are! You're an original! You're unique! No one else has your smile, your frown, your walk, your laugh, your brilliant ideas. So instead of always comparing yourself to other kids, be proud of your specialness. If people think you're silly, let them! You'll be the one they'll be wanting an autograph from in 20 years at your high school reunion because, by then, you'll be a famous comedian! Instead of telling yourself how stupid or ugly or clumsy or unpopular you are, give yourself your props. After all, if you don't hold yourself in high esteem and if you don't like you, why should anybody else?

I am special, and I feel good about myself.

January 4

I went through a lot from age 15 to about 19 years. I was very young. I used to hurt so badly that I'd ask God, "Why? What have I done to deserve this?"
—Janet Jackson

Being a teenager is not an easy job—even if you're Janet Jackson. As a teen, Janet had it going on! She was on TV and her brothers, The Jacksons, were the bomb. But everybody, from the best-looking girl and guy in school, to the worst-looking girl and guy, has problems. All families, those who don't seem to have enough money, those with just enough to get by and those with mad money, have their own special problems. If you're unhappy about your life or your family situation, you may wonder just like Janet did, *What have I done to deserve this?* You know what? You're not going to get all the answers now. Some things won't make sense until you're older. For now, though, you have to learn how not to hurt so much. And you have t6 understand that life will make more sense to you the longer you live it.

As I mature, I understand things better.

January 5

I wasn't blessed with a lot of natural talent. Nothing came easy for me. I had to work to perfect my skills.
—Mike Piazza

Are you determined to make all *A's* next semester? Have you decided that nothing is going to stop you from starting on the varsity football team next year? If so, you've also decided to work hard to achieve these goals. People who are successful and who achieve great things don't do so overnight, even though it may seem that way. They've put in many hours of hard work to become as good as or as smart as they are. The next time you see someone doing something and you think about how lucky that person is to be as good as they are, think again. They weren't born knowing how to score 40 points in a basketball game. They weren't born knowing how get all the test questions right. They worked hard to get where they are. You can too!

I am willing to work hard for what I want in life.

January 6

You have a brain, use it!
                    —Salt of Salt-N-Pepa

All da ladies in the house say "I can do math too!
Sci-ence is for me!" All da fellas in the house say
"She can do math too! Sci-ence is for she!" For
years we've heard boys are better than girls at math
and science. It ain't true. Girls, you can do anything
including complicated math problems and chemical
equations. And you can learn anything including
laws of physics and scientific theorems! It starts with
believing you can. Next, you pay attention in class,
and you make sure you understand what the teacher
is saying *before* you leave. Then, you do your
homework and you ace the test! You can study
biology, physics or math in college if that's your
choice. It's like anything else in life, once you've
determined that math and science are for you, you let
nothing and no one stop you from making them
yours. Not the teachers, not yourself, no one!

I can do math too! Science is for me!

January 7

I did things to please someone else; my priorities were him first, me second. But I'm changing.
—Sandra Bullock

Hey girlfriend, forget about that man for a minute, and think about you! Sure, it's fun to be with your man, but what have you done for *you* lately? If you are not the most important person in your life, ask yourself, who is? After you've answered that question, answer this one, Why? You've got to make you the focus of your life because if you don't care about yourself—I mean really care—no one else will. And remember, you're responsible for your happiness, not some man! Begin loving you and focusing on you while you're young. It's okay to have a man. It's okay to love your man, but don't ever forget you come first!

I am good to myself!

January 8

Everybody wants to look a certain way and have a certain body.
—Eddie Murphy

The reason everybody wants to look good and have a great body is because we think if we look good, boys will want to date us or girls will want to go out with us. The bottom line is you want people to approve of you and like you. Well, it's true that of us want to go out with people who are good-looking. And you're perfectly normal if you want your peers to approve of you. Just don't forget that although you need approval from your friends, you also need your own approval. You need to feel good about yourself if you're ever going to make it in life. You need to feel good about yourself no matter how you look. And the more you can accept who you are and how you look, the better you'll feel about yourself!

I love and approve of myself.

January 9

The bad thing about trouble is that trouble can be fun.
But trouble can also be dangerous.
—Queen Latifah

Getting into trouble can be fun. You can get a rush from doing things that are dangerous or things that could get you into trouble or things your parents, the police and some of your friends would call stupid! But as you mature, you'll understand you don't have to do stupid things to get a rush. You'll find more constructive ways to deal with boredom. You'll spend your time doing things that make you happy that aren't also dangerous and that won't also cause you some serious trouble. In the meantime, please don't do something so stupid and so dangerous that it costs you your life and your chance at growing up.

Even though I get a rush from getting into trouble, I know when to stop.

January 10

Yeah, I was cool. I smoked pot and blew coke. I experimented. But I stopped because I wanted to stay alive and make money, be somebody. And if I can do it, you can.

—Fernando Mateo

Fernando Mateo grew up in New York's Lower East Side. In high school, Fernando was made fun of. He struggled to fit in, and he began using drugs to try to fit in. To get away from drugs, Fernando dropped out of school and, soon thereafter, began working in the carpet business. After being publicly embarrassed by his boss for messing up some carpet, Fernando quit and went to work for another company. That job didn't work out either. So, at age 17 with a $2,000 loan from his father, Fernando opened Carpet Fashions. Nearly 13 years later, Fernando began giving back. Just before Christmas, Fernando decided to get people to trade their guns for toys. He gave out twenty-five, $100 Toys R Us gift certificates to anyone who turned in a gun to the 34th Precinct in New York City—no questions asked.

I am somebody, and I'm making the most of my life.

January 11

Most kids don't see the relationship between what they learn in a math class and what they will be doing in life.

—Jaime Escalante

Have you ever bought clothes or shoes when they were 15%, 20% or 30% off? Did you know how much money you'd save before the cashier rang up your purchase? Did you ever wonder why the 24-second clock in the NBA is only 24 seconds? If you know how to add, subtract, multiply and divide, you can figure out how much money you save when the $150 pair of sneakers you've been wanting is 20% off. Twenty percent multiplied by 150 equals 30 (.20 x 150). Subtract $30 from $150 and give the cashier $120 for your sneakers. Back in 1954, NBA officials determined that when neither team stalled during the game, each would take 60 shots; therefore, 120 shots total would be taken during an NBA game. There are 2,880 seconds in a 48-minute game (48 minutes x 60 seconds = 2,880). One-hundred twenty shots taken divided by 2,880 seconds, equals 24 seconds— enough time for each team to take its 60 shots.

I use mathematics to help me get through life.

January 12

I don't know any other way of living than striving for my absolute best.
> —Dominique Dawes

Do you know what your best is in English class, math class, on the track field, on the basketball court, on your part-time job? Here's a secret—*your best hasn't happened yet!* Each day you have another chance to prove what your best is. If you think you did the very best you could today or last week or last year, think again! You'll never really know what your best is until you stop trying to do better than you did before. Is it wrong to stop trying to reach a goal if you decide you would rather go after something else? Of course not! But when you wake up each day determined to do your very best, you're living life the way it was intended. Do things always go the way you want them to? Of course not! But wouldn't you rather be able to say, more times than not, "I did the best I could today!"

Each day, my best gets better!

January 13

Some birds fly off the tree limb just by their mothers telling them. Some birds like me need a little push.
—Craig Mack

Clean your room. Do your homework. Stay out of trouble. Blah, blah, blah! Does it feel like your parents are always telling you what to do and giving you that "little push" like Craig talks about? Your parents have to tell you what to do. *It's their job!* It's called guidance. They're preparing you to become an adult, just like the mother bird prepares her baby birds to leave the nest. So you can stop getting mad at your parents! Why? Because if they don't do their job, they'll be in some serious trouble! You may have your own ideas about what you do and don't want to do. But doing your homework now teaches discipline and good work habits for later. Being neat and clean now teaches you how to keep a clean house when you grow up. So remember, "do this, do that" really means, "I love you and I want the best for you, and *I'm just doing my job!*

When I accept my parents' guidance, I accept my parents' love.

January 14

I am not a role model. Parents should be role models.
—Charles Barkley

Charles is correct. Our parents took on the job of being our role models when we were born. But as you know, some parents aren't good role models. Parents who fuss and fight, parents who abuse drugs, parents who tell kids they're no good and parents who work all the time and ignore their kids aren't good role models. You can't change your parents. But you can change how you think and feel about yourself even if your parents are having their own problems. How? By understanding that there is something inside you called love. Love is a powerful force that can help you feel good about yourself even when things around you, whether at home, in school or in society are messed up. No, some parents aren't good role models, and some don't give kids the love they need. No matter what your parents do or don't do, remember you are a great kid! You are special! And you are filled with love!

I love and approve of myself.

January 15

When you love God, you can love yourself, you can love others.

—Evander Holyfield

Do you know God? Are you afraid of God? Mad at God? Excited about God? Do you even believe in God? By the time you become teenagers, you've developed some beliefs about God. Your beliefs are probably based on how you've been raised and what you've learn from those who've raised you. You may accept what you've been taught or you may not. If you have questions about God, you're not alone. If you don't believe in God or a higher power, you're not alone. If you want to know more about God, you're not alone. How do you learn more about God or a higher power? One way is to keep learning more about who you are and who you want to become. As you mature, you'll decide what makes sense to you about God. No matter what you think about God, you can believe Evander when he says you can't love anybody else until you first love you.

Each day I come to a greater understanding of myself and God.

January 16

We believe strongly in God and everything that revolves around Him.
> —Brian Dalyrimple of Soul IV
> Real

Some teens responses when asked their beliefs about God: I believe in God in a way, but I don't understand it. • I don't believe in God, but I believe in my father. My dad's the one who's been there, who's taken care of me, so that's God to me—my father. • I don't even know about God. God is mysterious. • Every time I think about God, I think about stop sinning. • He gives you the sense that there's a better place to go to and that dying's not such a bad thing. • The older I get the more I question hell. • I think God doesn't judge anybody, but I think the religion does. • I know there's a higher power out there somewhere that's gonna lead me somewhere, but I don't believe in the whole religion thing. • I believe in myself. • It just seems like every little single thing I do, you have to fear Him. • I've always been brought up to love God and believe in God, and that is a major part of my life. *Please finish the affirmation for yourself below.*

*I believe*_____

January 17

I used to be down and out. That's all I was, just sad. And for what? It takes so much energy to be negative.

—Mary J. Blige

What is energy? Energy is the stuff each of us is made of. Stuff? In this case, stuff is the molecules, called atoms, bopping around inside us. All of us have what's called an energy field. Our energy field is part of the energy field that exists in the universe. What universe? The wonderful universe that contains everything—you, me, the planets, the sun, the stars, the moon, everything! Each of us is part of the universe and we are all connected by the same energy that flows in and through all living things. When Mary says it takes so much energy to be negative, she's reciting a law of physics. It takes more energy to be angry and pissed off than it does to be happy and chilled out. Negative energy is bad for you. It can actually make you sick—sick with a headache, a stomachache, you name it! With positive energy, you can feel good and do good things.

I radiate positive energy.

January 18

The fact that I'm a black woman doing sports is nothing compared with what my ancestors have done. The least I can do to honor them is fulfill the dream I have.
—Robin Roberts

Robin Roberts has worked in radio and television in Mississippi, Atlanta and around the world for ESPN and ABC Sports. Her father was a Tuskegee Airman who rose to the rank of colonel in the Air Force. Her mother was a well-respected Mississippi educator. If your parents, grandparents, aunts and uncles have made the most of their lives, be proud of them, but don't try to compare yourself to them or compete with them. Don't put pressure on yourself to live up to your parents' or your relatives' accomplishments. Just do what Robin did—fulfill your own dreams! Draw strength from the fact that your parents or relatives have achieved great things, and know in your heart you can also achieve great things. It's good to honor your ancestors by making the most of your life. But it's one thing to honor and another thing to compare and compete.

Each day I honor my ancestors by making the most of my life.

January 19

She was a single parent. I saw that determination in her eyes. She wasn't going to let her kids down. She did whatever it took.
—Sheryl Swoopes

Are you being reared by a single mother or father? Is your single parent working two jobs to support you and your brothers and sisters? You've been taught right from wrong, and you've been told to stay away from drugs and gangs. Still, some of you get into gangs and start doing or dealing drugs anyway. When your mother or father finds out about this, he may get angry—she may even cry. Sometimes, they help you avoid trouble. Other times, the cops and the court system get you first. Then, it's juvenile detention, placement, probation officers and all those trips to court. If you don't realize it now, you will later: Your single parent is doing the best he or she can for you! You may want to have more money. You may be angry because your father is not around or because your mother abandoned you, but disobeying your parent leads only to trouble.

I understand that my single parent is doing the best he or she can for me.

January 20

We decided we weren't going to let anyone limit us by telling us we couldn't do something.
—Wyclef Jean of the Fugees

Have you heard the story about the eagle and the prairie chickens? Someone found an eagle's egg, and, by mistake, put it in a prairie chicken's nest. The egg hatched with a brood of prairie chicks, and the baby eagle grew up with the chicks. The eagle clucked liked they clucked, cackled like the chicks cackled and flapped its wings, flying just a few feet into the air, just like a prairie chicken. One day, the young eagle saw a bird with mad flying skills and asked who it was. "That's an eagle," came the reply. "The baddest bird on the planet." "Wouldn't it be great if I could soar like that," the eagle then asked. "Don't even think about it," a chick shot back. "You and me are just a bunch of prairie chickens. We could never do that." The young eagle believed the chick's lie and never again thought about flying. It went to its grave thinking it was a prairie chicken.

Nothing and no one can keep me from my dream.

January 21

Once we see the grass isn't greener over on the other side of the fence then we'll all be happier.
—Jonathan Taylor Thomas

While you're spending time wanting what someone else has and being miserable, you're probably not using the special gifts only you have. No one can do what you do the way you do it. Because you have something special, there's really no reason to be jealous of what others have. Like Jonathan says, the grass may look greener at someone else's house, but remember, nobody's house is perfect. That may be hard for you to believe, especially if you think you've been cheated by life or by God or by your circumstances! If you think you've been cheated, you've got to change your thinking! Develop more self-confidence, begin to know just how special you are and start using your special talents. Once you start using your talents and living up to your potential, you won't have time to feel cheated. And you won't waste time looking at other people's grass.

I am special and I have stuff I can work

January 22

Yeah, my childhood was tough, but bad situations make people stronger.
—Alonzo Mourning

After Alonzo Mourning's parents divorced when he was 11, he ended up in foster care. Alonzo lived with several foster-care parents before being sent to a woman named Fanny Threet. Alonzo stayed with Threet until he left for Georgetown University. Mourning could have given up and given in because of the hardship he faced as a child, but he didn't! It's not easy when you grow up in a messed-up home or when bad things happen when you're a kid. But bad things do happen, and some homes are messed up. The key is to never give up hope. You don't believe in hope? Talk to NBA superstar Alonzo Mourning. Talk to Jim Abbott, Major League pitcher who pitched for years despite having been born with only one hand. Talk to someone you know who's overcome hardship and turned his life or her life around. Then, ask yourself if you're really ready to give up and give in.

I am a stronger person because of the rough times I've had in my life.

January 23

It is our birthright to know who we are and how special we are. If we don't know who we are, we'll always feel envy, jealousy, fear and insecurity about our beauty and our power.

—Marilyn Youngbird

Who are you? Each of us, whether we're black, brown, yellow or white are spiritual, mental and physical beings. We are spiritual and mental beings living in physical bodies. Too many of us though, neglect our spirits. We eat, exercise, read and study—activities that nourish our bodies and minds. But what about the spirit? If we're spiritual beings, we've got to be about spiritual things. How do we do this? We first understand that there is a power badder than you, me, the U.S. army, the drug dealer, the NBA player of the year, the priest, the top rap group, the highest paid fashion model and anyone else you can think of in a billion years. That power, called by different names, Allah, Higher Power, the Creator, Higher Intelligence, the Universe, Spirit, God lives inside you because it created you! Now do you know who you are?

January 24

I've always known where I wanted to go in life. I've never let anything deter me. This is my purpose. It will unfold.
—Tiger Woods

Everybody has a purpose in life. Some people are supposed to be rappers. Some writers. Some are supposed to be lawyers. Some cosmetologists. Some are supposed to be police officers. Some doctors. Some are supposed to go into business for themselves. If you don't know what your purpose is, don't worry! You don't have to know this moment or by tomorrow or by next year or even by the time you graduate from school. Some people, people like Tiger, know their purpose at age 3. Some people don't find out until they're 40. Others die without ever having known why they lived! But if you stay connected with your inner wisdom and your higher power, you will discover your purpose. And like Tiger says, when you know what your purpose is—*it will unfold.*

My inner wisdom and my higher power allow me to discover my purpose.

January 25

Have you had your break today?
> —McDonald's advertising slogan

Today, you're going on break! Have you been wearing your smile upside down lately? Today you're going to wear it right-side up! Have you been mad at your best friend and not speaking to him or her? Well, today you're taking a break, and you're going to speak to your best friend. Been hanging out on the corner? Making that paper? Well, today, take a break. Have you been depressed lately? Feeling down and out? Not today! Say to yourself, "Today I'm on break!" Instead of being sad all day, find one thing you can be happy about and concentrate on that. Instead of getting angry at your teacher, refrain from anger. Instead of getting into a fight, walk away from it. Instead of cussing someone out, say something nice to them. And if you like the way you're feeling tomorrow when your break is over, take another one!

Today, I let nothing and no one keep me from being happy and at peace.

January 26

The racism, the sexism, I never let it be my problem. It's their problem, If I see a door comin' my way, I'm knockin' it down. And if I can't knock down the door, I'm sliding through the window.
—Rosie Perez

Yo! Yo! Yo! Yo! Racism is only a problem for you if you let it be. If someone doesn't like you because you're Hispanic or black or Asian, it's *their* problem. If a teacher or a classmate or whoever tries to make you feel bad or inferior because they want to believe they're better than you, tell them to step off! It ain't happening. Not here. Their attempt to feel good about themselves by thinking they're better than you is their problem. It will stay their problem unless you begin believing they're better, smarter or more valuable than you. They're not! The way to fight racism and prejudice is not by sitting around talking about how racist America is or by doggin' out white people. The way to overcome racism is to believe in yourself and do great things! It's only when you make racism your problem, instead of their problem, that racism beats you!

Racism has no power over me.

January 27

You think there's joy in a high because it feels good temporarily. But it feels good less and less often so you've got to do it more and more often. It ain't your friend.

—Whoopi Goldberg

Why do some teens start using drugs? To deal with stress maybe. As a teenager, your hormones have begun flipping, you're going through physical changes and you alternate between being optimistic about your life and the future and being pissed off with society and everybody in it! In other words, you go through changes. *And changes can be stressful.* Some of you turn to drugs when you're stressed. You may start with alcohol or weed then move up to crack or heroin. But drugs don't cure stress! Like Whoopi says, drugs give you a temporary high. *Learning how to deal with the changes you go through is the cure for stress.* Daily meditations will help you to better handle the changes so you don't have to get all stressed out in the first place! On the next page, you'll get some ideas on how to meditate.

I am learning how to deal with the stress in my life in a healthy way.

January 28

I try to be as spiritually centered and as focused as I can be, to create an atmosphere that is going to be positive and manifest positive things in my life.
—LL Cool J

What does it mean to be spiritually centered? It means you understand your spirit controls your mind and body. Your spirit gives you life and, unlike the mind and body, your spirit never dies. Meditating for 20 minutes by concentrating on one sound—like the sound of yourself breathing—helps you become spiritually centered. When meditating, don't try to stop your thoughts. You can't. But you can ignore them and concentrate on a repetitive sound. For instance, when you think about what so-and-so did, you don't get pissed off or sad or ready to fight. And when you have happy thoughts, you don't stay with them either. Happy, sad, crazy or bad, ignore them! Meditating lets you connect with your spirit and it helps you understand yourself better. After you've been meditating for a while, you'll notice you don't stress things like you used to. You let go of more.

I am spiritually centered.

January 29

Everybody likes money. Money buys comfort. But no, not happiness. Happiness comes from another place.

—Sinbad

What does money mean to you? Does your family live comfortably or do your parents struggle to pay their bills? Like Sinbad says, money can give you access to certain comforts, but having a million dollars will not make you or anyone else happy. Money can't keep you from feeling lonely or afraid or unloved. Money is something you exchange for something else. You exchange money for clothes, sneakers, cars, concert tickets, movie tickets, burgers, fries, etc. You cannot exchange money for love or happiness or inner peace. You cannot buy happiness or put it on layaway or pay for it with your credit card. Many of you have decided you want to be rich when you grow up because you think being rich will make you happy. You think being rich and having more money than you can count will solve all your problems. It won't.

My happiness does not come from money, it comes from inside me.

January 30

I try not to focus on anything negative so it doesn't become more than it is.
—Larenz Tate

Focusing on negative stuff brings harmful stress into your life. But stress is meant to help you, not hurt you. When you're in danger, something called your stress response causes your muscles to get ready for action, your energy to increase and your heart to beat faster. You felt your heart beating faster the last time you were really afraid. But if you're always stressed and worrying about stuff, you'll start feeling tired, pissed and upset. Have you ever had a hard time doing your homework, and you started thinking, *I can never get this stuff right.* Have you ever walked by some people who laughed as you passed them? Did you think, *I know they're laughing at me!* Word! It's not true you *never* get stuff right! And just because somebody laughs, it doesn't mean they're laughing at you. Try not to be so negative. Stop blowing things up and instead think positive thoughts.

When a negative thought pops into my head, I replace it with a positive thought.

January 31

If you are tenacious and think positive, you can do anything.

—Lela Rochon

To be tenacious means you have to put your hands over your ears when people try to put you down and tell you what you can't do. When you're tenacious, you don't give up when things get rough, rather, you stay strong and fight 'til the end. When you're tenacious, you don't take no for an answer, and you look at obstacles as challenges to be overcome. When you're tenacious, you're persistent, resolute, determined, serious, enduring, unswerving, unyielding, indefatigable, steadfast, persevering, inexorable, relentless and fierce! You can be tenacious on the basketball court. You can be unyielding when running 100 meters. You can be determined, persistent and resolute when pursuing scholarship money for college. Word! You would want to be tenacious any time you decide to go for what you really want in life!

I am tenacious, I am fierce!

February 1

Let's recognize the reality of a talented new generation, righteous in their thinking, pumped up on pride and ready to take on the world.
　　　　　—Will Smith

You are part of the talented new generation, but what are you doing with yourself? The media tell us one thing about what some of you are doing. But the media don't always tell the truth! Even though there's only a small percentage of African-American and Latino youth who gang bang and deal drugs, a small percentage of several million is still too many. How many of you are righteous thinkers? Those of you who think of girls as bitches and ho's aren't! How many of you are pumped up on pride? If you don't know what you have to be proud of—find out! Oftentimes, you're not taught in schools the truth about your history. But there are books out there that speak the truth. The second section of this book speaks the truth about history. Are you ready to take on the world? You don't take on the world with 9 millimeters, knives and blunts. You take on the world with righteous thinking and a proud spirit!

I am talented, proud and righteous.

February 2

In some neighborhoods, people were expected to go to college. But in my neighborhood, people were expected to go to prison.
—Charles Dutton

What are your parents' expectations for you? What are your expectations for yourself? If you remember that you get in life exactly what you expect, you'll probably start expecting big things. Sometimes, your parents have unreasonable expectations. They may want you to grow up and be exactly like them. If they're doctors or lawyers, they may want you to be a doctor or a lawyer, even if that's not what you want. Or they may be pushing you, along with coaches, to become a professional athlete or an Olympic gold medalist at a young age. Sometimes parents push *too* hard. Other times, parents may not expect enough of you. But none of you should expect that you're headed for prison, unless that's where you want to end up. Whatever *you* decide you want to do in life, remember to always expect the best from yourself.

Whatever I am guided to do will be a success.

February 3

I know I'm a good person.
—Faith Evans

Do you know how good you are? How special you
are? Do you know how much potential you have?
Do you know there's something special you're
supposed to accomplish in this here life? If you
know these things, you're no doubt trying to figure
out how to make the most of your unlimited
potential. You're already thinking about how to
fulfill your purpose in life. If you don't know how
good, valuable and special you are, you're probably
struggling through life. When you don't know how
good and special you are, you do all kinds of crazy
things to try to feel good and special. Begin
eliminating all the lies you've told yourself about how
bad you are. Stop telling yourself you're not as good
as others. Know and really believe in your beauty
and your specialness. Recognize your value to
society. Why? Because you are a good person. You
are special.

I am valuable. I am special.

February 4

I'm such a perfectionist, everything I do I think is wrong.

—Anfernee Hardaway

It would be nice to get 100 on every test you ever take in life. Or would it? Since no one has ever done that, we'll never know. Too many of you think you have to be perfect or else you're no good. Some of you think if you do everything perfectly, Dad will stop beating Mom, and you'll have a happy family. Others of you think if you get good grades and never get into trouble, your parents will love you more. Does it work? Only you can answer that. But love and acceptance and approval should not depend on you doing everything perfectly. Some of you have parents who love you *unconditionally*. When you mess up, you're disciplined, but you're still loved! And you're told that you're a great kid who did something stupid or wrong. The power that created you also accepts you and loves you *no matter what you do!* You don't have to try to be perfect!

My higher power loves me as I am.

February 5

I have long ago reconciled myself to the fact that some people will never accept me simply because of the color of my skin.

—Montel Williams

Some of you have met up with teachers and professors who don't seem to accept you or care whether you succeed. If you're black and those teachers are white, you may assume they don't care because they're prejudiced or racist. Well, what if they are racist? Racism and prejudice will confront you throughout your life. But remember, racism has no power over you. Yes, racism and prejudice make you angry. It's normal to become angry. But you can't stay angry. Why? Because anger takes away your ability to become the person you were meant to become. The way you deal with teachers who don't seem to care whether you make it, for whatever reasons, is to make it in spite of them! Show them your greatness! Show them *your* intelligence. Show them that nothing, not even their negative attitudes, will keep you from succeeding.

Nothing and no one will keep me from being successful in school.

February 6

Life doesn't necessarily get better, you get better at life.

—Sade

If you thought it was the end of the world yesterday because you asked a girl if she wanted a man and she said, "not you," then you're just like any other teenage boy who ever lived. If you thought you'd never get over finding out your best friend had been messing with your man behind your back, you're just like any other teenage girl who ever lived. You're in the early and middle stages of what is called the growth and maturation process. You're not yet mature enough to understand that getting cut from the football team or not making the cheerleading team is not the end of the world even though it may feel like it to you. When you're feeling bad or depressed or like your world is all messed up, ask your higher power for guidance and strength. Like Sade says, there will always be rough times, but as you mature, you'll be able to handle them better.

Each day, I am a more mature person.

February 7

I'm just me, and that's all I want to be.
—Tevin Campbell

You can only be you! And if there are some things about you that make you wish you were someone else, you can change those things. Maybe you don't like how you look. Well, you can change your looks, and you can do so without paying a plastic surgeon $5,000. How? *Change your attitude!* When you lose your depressed, nasty or fearful attitude and get a cheerful, friendly attitude, cheerful, friendly people will want to hang with you. People will notice a change in you, and they'll feel more comfortable approaching you. When that happens, you won't want to be anybody else. If you're bothered because you're overweight, changing how and what you eat and exercising regularly can help you to lose weight. But that new attitude works wonders here too—*for real!* Begin to love yourself no matter how you look, and you'll begin to notice a difference in how you look and in how others look at you.

I love who I am and who I am becoming.

February 8

Life is a gift from God.
                —Pedro Zamora

You are phat! You've got the juice. You are *the* one!
You rock! You make things happen. You have mad
skills. You are wonderful! Your future is bright!
You've got the power. You are a good person. You
get things done. You are super funky fresh. No one
can do it like you do it. You make the grade.
Nobody does it better than you. You're number one.
You really are all that! You are love. You are life!
You are a gift from God! A gift from God? Yes.
You are a gift from God...to the world!

I am a gift from God...to the world!

February 9

If you want to stop young people from doing gangsta rap, then change the social conditions from which that comes.

—Benjamin Chavis

In the 1950s, 60s and 70s, freedom fighters named Cesar Chavez, Fannie Lou Hamer, Malcolm X, Delores Huerta, Vernon Johns, Ruben Salazar, and Dr. Martin Luther King, Jr., did change social conditions. If, as a group, Latinos and African-Americans wait for others to make things better, you'll be waiting forever. Racism is their problem. Making your communities and your lives better is on you. Of course, there are things you can't control. You can't stop a racist policeman from detaining you because he thinks you're a drug dealer even when you're not. But there are things you *can* control. You can stop blaming everyone else for the mess you create for yourself. You can start believing you have a future in America. You can become a freedom fighter by freeing yourself from whatever it is you *think* is holding you back.

I am changing my life for the better.

February 10

Hype: Deception, put-on. Extravagant promotion or advertising.
>—Dictionary definition

Not so long ago, Public Enemy told us not to believe the hype. But every day, we do believe what we see and hear on TV, the radio and in the movies. What's up with that? The reason so many of us believe the hype is because we haven't taken the time to really examine the hype. It's time! Drugs, sex and relationships are often misrepresented on TV and in film. Sure sex can be great, being in a relationship can make you feel mad good and drugs produce a high that also feels good. But drugs can also kill you! And if you're using drugs to get a high, you're wasting your money because you could be high without drugs. Sex, in an intimate, caring relationship allows adults to grow deeper together and to build trust. Having sex to make you feel good for five minutes or because someone is pressuring you is having sex for the wrong reasons. Don't believe the hype!

I understand the difference between hype and what's real.

February 11

If you wanted to get respected by your peers and liked by the ladies, you had to be a gangster or an athlete or a rapper.

—Kid of Kid N' Play

Our world would be a sad place if it were true that the only options for young African-American and Latino men are gang banging, rapping or kicking, throwing or bouncing a ball. Fellas, you shouldn't let the ladies or your homies tell you you're nothing unless you're doing what they say. Decide for yourself there's nothing wrong with being a good student and getting good grades. You decide there's nothing wrong with respecting girls. You decide you can do anything you want in life. And remember, you determine your tomorrow by what you do today. You don't have to wait until adulthood to decide you're going to make the most out of the life you've been given. You don't have to wait until you're an adult to figure out that being black or Hispanic is not synonymous with being a gangsta, an athlete or a rapper.

I decide what's right for me.

February 12

A relaxed attitude lengthens a man's life.
—Proverbs 14:30

When you sit quietly in the morning, you can prepare for a great day. Sitting quietly with your back straight and your eyes closed helps you become centered. Twenty minutes of deep breathing and concentrating on your breaths helps you connect with your spirit. It's called meditating. Here's how it works: when you concentrate on the sound of your own breathing you don't pay attention to the thoughts you're having. You can't stop thinking, but you can ignore your many thoughts. When you meditate, you may think about something that would normally make you sad, but because you ignore the thought, you don't get sad. You concentrate on one sound over and over and over, and you chill. After you've been meditating for a while, you'll notice you don't stress things the way you used to. You let go of more.

Each day I am more and more relaxed.

February 13

Acceptance. That's one of the principles of recovery.
　　　　　　　—John Lucas

Before you can begin to solve your problems, you've got to accept that you have problems. If you're strung out on alcohol or drugs, you've got a serious problem. If you're addicted to sex, or fighting or junk food or food in general, you've also got a serious problem. The first step in getting rid of your addiction is to accept that you are addicted. After that, you have to understand that you're using alcohol or drugs or sex or fighting or food to relieve tension and to help you feel good. For some, that tension and stress is normal teenage stress. Others of you are trying to relieve deep-rooted stress and pain that's been building since you were children. If you're already addicted to something that's bad for you, accept that you've got a problem and get help! If you're thinking about using drugs, alcohol or anything else bad to make you feel better—don't!

I own up to my problems, and I take positive steps toward solving them.

February 14

Teachers don't expect much from Hispanic students,
so students don't try hard in school.
                    —Dr. Roberto Cruz

Do you like your teachers? Do you like some of
them, but not others? If you have teachers you don't
like, is it because you think they don't like you?
Have they said things to you like, "Why don't you go
back to Puerto Rico," or "Why don't you go back to
Mexico." It's true that some teachers think because
you're Mexican or Puerto Rican or Dominican or
Panamanian or Cuban you're not as smart as other
kids. You can't change your teachers' wack thinking.
But you can show them how wrong they are by being
as smart as you can be. And you can change you if
that's what it takes. What do you think about you?
Do you think you're not as smart as other kids? Do
you think that because you're Hispanic, you can't
learn what other kids can? If so, you're wrong just
like some of your teachers. Always remember, you're
as smart as you think you are!

I am intelligent.

February 15

I've never put any limitations on myself.
—Debbie Allen

When you say you can't do it because you're a girl or because you're not smart enough or because it's only for white people, you are limiting yourself. Oh, you'd never say those things. Well, have you ever thought them? If so, it is time to begin banishing all negative, limiting, self-defeating thoughts from your mind. You can start by getting rid of all those awful, negative words taking up space in your brain. Words like *can't, but* and *should.* What's wrong with can't, but and should? First of all, you can! And when you're doing everything you can do, there's never a need for should, as in "I should be doing this or "I should have done that." Instead of reaching for a convenient "but" all the time, why not spend your mental energy figuring out how you can get the job done instead of wracking your brain trying to find a good excuse because you're afraid to try.

I release all negative thoughts from my mind.

February 16

I think violence is a learned behavior and getting along is a skill, just like basketball. You need to practice.

—Dr. Deborah Prothrow-Stith

Stop the violence! Anger is a normal human emotion but it doesn't have to lead to violence! Instead of hunting down a classmate and stabbing her because she's been spreading rumors about you, "squash it!" You can also learn to remain chilled when your parents yell at you. How? By learning how to react *appropriately* to criticism. When your parents criticize your behavior many of you think they're saying "You suck. You're no good." Wrong! Your behavior sucks! Your behavior was no good. When criticism hurts, tell yourself, "I love and approve of myself. I am a good person." Dr. Prothrow-Stith, a physician and assistant dean at the Harvard School of Public Health, created a violence prevention program that teaches you how to express anger appropriately. If your school or community organization doesn't have her program or one like it, ask them to get it.

Each day, I am less violent.

February 17

I went to three different funerals for three different friends when I was 13. My best friend was shot dead right in front of my eyes.

—Matty Rich

When someone we love is murdered, we feel shock, denial, anger and sadness. We also feel as if we have no control over what happens, and we no longer feel safe. When a teenage friend or a brother, sister or cousin is killed, we're often left feeling we could be next. When someone you love is murdered, you may feel as though there is no hope and "What's the use?" It's okay to cry. It's okay to be sad. You may also feel like you want revenge. It's okay to feel vengeful, but it's not okay to try to get revenge. Whatever you're feeling, talk over your feelings with people you love. One thing to remember is that the power that created you lives inside you, even when things seem hopeless. Your higher power will get you through your brother's murder. Your higher power will get you through your sister's murder, your cousin's murder, your friend's murder—if you allow it to.

My higher power keeps me safe and secure.

February 18

We must develop and maintain the capacity to forgive. He who is devoid of the power to forgive is devoid of the power to love.
—Dr. Martin Luther King Jr.

Everybody has a rough time forgiving others when they think others have done them wrong. But when you don't forgive others, it messes you up! Holding on to anger and resentment will make you sick. Not forgiving others keeps *you* down not the people you're mad at. Don't try to be forgiving on your own. Ask your higher power for help. *Forgive* your parents for seeming to care more about their careers than about you. *Forgive* your father for running out on you when you were 4. *Forgive* the person who caused you and your family so much pain. *Forgive* yourself for causing your mother pain when you started running with the wrong crowd. When we forgive others, we stop being angry at them for what we think they've done to us. When we forgive ourselves, we stop being angry at ourselves for what we think we've done to ourselves and to others.

Each day, I am more forgiving.

February 19

If you don't teach children that they're valuable, then they don't learn to value anything.
—Umar Lambright

That's right. Your parents should tell you how valuable you are! Well, sometimes they don't! Sometimes they're too busy working or too rapped up in their own lives to pay attention to you and show you how valuable you are. Sometimes they're so busy that they neglect giving you the love you deserve. So now what? Because you weren't made to feel valuable, you steal, kill and abuse your bodies? You can do that, but what does it get you? It gets you in jail, dead or HIV infected. Word! *You are valuable!* You are unique. There is no one on this earth who has your exact same features, thoughts, or dreams. You were created special. You do have something valuable to give to the world. If you haven't yet figured out what that is, don't worry—you will. For now though, recognize your value and your specialness. You do count! You are valuable!

I am valuable. I am special!

February 20

We were in the poorhouse. I would walk up to the playground and see a guy open up his trench coat with 1,000 syringes.
—Leonardo DiCaprio

Some of you live in what are considered "bad" neighborhoods. Drug dealers stand on street corners. People shoot guns. Older kids and adults are trying to get you to sell or buy drugs! It's hard when everybody else in the neighborhood is doing something and you're not. It's easy to start doing what everybody else is doing if you're the only one not doing it. But if *everybody* does the wrong thing and no one stands up for right, how will your neighborhood survive? If at age 13, you start hanging out with 16- and 17-year-olds caught up in alcohol and drugs, then what's going to happen to your little brother who wants to be just like you? What will happen to your 8-year-old sister who wants to act just like her big 13-year-old sister?

I am doing the right things even when everyone else is doing the wrong things.

February 21

Violence is love gone crazy.
                    —Ruben Blades

Violent people are people who have lost their love!
When people lose their love, they flip! And they flip
because they're afraid. There are two emotions, love
and fear, that determine all of our other emotions.
So, whenever you're happy or confident or feeling
safe and secure, it's because you're feeling the love!
And whenever you're angry or sad or jealous or
embarrassed or insecure or feeling resentment and
hatred, it's because you're afraid, and you're feeling
fear. When any of us is afraid, we've forgotten that
love is always there for us, telling us not to be afraid.
The only way to increase the peace and stop the
violence is for each of us to get our love back! If
your love has flipped, unflip it. Start by loving
yourself no matter what. Once you get your love on,
you can squash the fear that can lead to anger, which
can lead to violence.

My love is greater than my fears.

February 22

Who knows how to handle a child like that?
>—Katharine Kinkel, Kip Kinkel's
> grandmother

It is alleged that Kip Kinkel murdered four people.
The 15-year-old is said to have murdered his parents
at home, then gone to school and murdered two
classmates. About two dozen more students were
injured. Kip's grandmother said that Kip's father told
her he'd given up on trying to straighten Kip out.
Given up. Listed below is a phone number you can
call when you feel like you want to give up. The
people who answer the phone will never give up on
you, even if everyone else has. Why? Because they
know you don't really want your parents to give up
on you even though you've done everything you
could think of to push them away. They also know
you don't really want to die, but that you're in so
much pain. They know. They know.

The Covenant House's 9 Line............800-999-9999

February 23

When I was in high school, I cared about more than getting a date or making the team. Your teen years are a time when you deal with some deep issues.
—Jared Leto

Jared is correct! All teens deal with some real deep issues. The trick to dealing with these real deep issues is to understand that *there is no trick!* There's just the dealing. You can run away from the issues facing you, but that won't solve anything. When you run, the things you're running from are right there with you! You run away because you're afraid. Everybody is afraid of something. And when you're afraid you feel that ache in the pit of your stomach. But the only way to overcome your fears is to face up to them. When you have faith in a higher power, you can face up to them! Ask your higher power for the courage to face up to your fears so that you can deal with your issues. And after you ask, listen! Feel! And don't be afraid of what you hear or feel.

I deal with the issues facing me, and I trust my higher power to help me.

February 24

Never give up hope, because there are people out there who care, even though at first it may not look that way.

—Carmella Thomas

When Carmella Thomas was 11, she ran away from home. She repeatedly ran away from her alcoholic and abusive parents until the state placed her in foster care. When her foster-care insurance ran out on her 18th birthday, she spent the night in a homeless shelter. She spent the next two years in a shelter, but she also took classes at Milwaukee Tech, got her high school diploma and looked out for the kids at the shelter. A woman who worked with homeless people saw Carmella's work with the kids and took Carmella into her home. At age 20, Carmella got a job with the City of Milwaukee creating youth councils in housing projects and working with violence prevention programs. Carmella was scared when she was on the streets and on her own, but she didn't let her fears get the best of her. And she never gave up hope! She overcame her fears and found the help she needed.

I know that there are people out there who care and who can help me.

February 25

God is within me.
                    —Debbi Morgan

The best gift you can give yourself is to take some time to connect with the God within you. It doesn't matter what you call it, it matters only that you hook up with it. You don't have to go to a church building to hook up with it because it's inside you. And you don't have to get someone else to help you find it because you own it. All you have to do is give it its props. Once you've connected with your internal power source, chill! Connecting with God and being spiritual is not as hard as you may think. Being spiritual means striving to feel God, or in others words—*love*—in everything and in everyone. Everyone is spiritual because our spirits give each of us life. You become more spiritual by staying in constant connection and constant communication with your spirit within.

I am spiritually connected with the God within me.

February 26

Right now, if you speak proper English and get *A's* in school, you're considered a white boy. It ain't down, it ain't cool, and it ain't black."
—Spike Lee

Being smart and getting good grades are *not* bad things! I know some of your classmates will give you much hell because you're smart. But did you ever stop to think about why they're doing that? Could it be they feel inferior because they believe they're dumb? Could it be when they get around you, *Ms. All A's* and *Mr. College Bound*, they want you to feel as dumb as they do? Well, they can get good grades too! They're not dumb; they only think they are. As long as they think they're dumb, they'll be too afraid to try because they've already convinced themselves they'd fail. That's on them. It's on you to be proud not ashamed of your intelligence and your good grades. Don't allow anyone, not even your best friend, to make you feel bad because you're doing well.

I am smart and proud of it!

February 27

The one who asks questions doesn't lose his way.
—Akan Proverb

What keeps you from asking questions in class or at an assembly? Fear? The feeling that your classmates will think you're stupid if you show you don't know something by asking about it? Well, asking about something you know nothing about is the only way to learn! When you want to find out about a guy or a girl you're interested in, you start by asking questions, don't you? And you don't care about looking stupid, do you? If you're afraid of looking "stupid" by asking questions in class, ask yourself why. The one who asks questions is the smart one, not the dumb one. If anyone has ever told you you're stupid or dumb or you'll never amount to anything, you need to check yourself and make sure you didn't believe those lies! If you did believe them, you need to reprogram your thinking so you become smart enough to know that the only stupid question is the one that isn't asked.

It's okay for me to ask questions in class.

February 28

I think every day you've got to learn something new.
— Yo-Yo Ma

Some of you have a hard time learning new things because you have a learning disability. If you have dyslexia, the letters in words seem to jump around the page when you try to read. And when you speak, you may reverse words and say hard when you mean soft or up when you mean down. If you suffer from a learning disability, you also have trouble taking in information. And you may tell yourself you're stupid or slow. You're not! Most kids with learning disabilities have average or above-average intelligence. And because parents and teachers know how smart you really are, they may think you're lazy or you don't care about school. But you do care! You do want to learn. If you're struggling with reading or with staying focused in class, tell your parents or your teachers. You may have a learning disability, and there is help for kids with learning disabilities.

I am intelligent even though learning may not come easy for me.

February 29

One should not rely on appearances.
Uno nunca debe confiarse en las apariencias.
—Mexican saying

You've heard the saying, "You can't judge a book by its cover." Well, when you form opinions about someone based on their looks, you often misjudge them. You think because someone is cute or good-looking they're also smart, or if someone is just average-looking or what you consider ugly, they're dumb. You judge people on how they look, or where they live or where they were born or how they talk before you get to know them and discover what's really up with them. But the person whom you think is ugly could also be the person who would be a true friend and stick with you in good times and in bad. But you'd never know that if you never bothered to become friends with them just because they didn't look a certain way! Remember, it's not what's on the outside of a person that matters most. It's what's inside—inside their mind and inside their heart.

I get to know people before I form opinions about them.

March 1

Money doesn't buy peace of mind.
—Babyface

Money can buy you a car, a house, Air Jordans,
Reeboks, Tommy Hilfiger pants, a Cross Colours
shirt, Boss jeans, a STARTER jacket, tickets to the
concert, a ticket to the football game, compact discs,
video games, cassette tapes, a haircut, hair spray, a
burger, a double burger, etc., etc., etc. Money cannot
buy you love. Money cannot buy you happiness.
Money cannot buy you a loving spirit. Money cannot
buy you the perfect boyfriend. Money cannot buy
you the perfect girlfriend. Money cannot buy you a
life where you'll never be afraid of anything or
anyone. Like Babyface says, money does not buy
peace of mind.

I am at peace with myself and the world.

March 2

When the status of life is gauged only by consumer goods and products, if you cannot have the product, you will kill for it.

—Toni Morrison

Many of you hear adults talk about priorities. A priority is something you put first in importance, position or preference. If at a young age, you decide it's more important to look good than to be a good person, then you've established certain priorities for yourself. Every teenager has wanted to look good, be down and fit in. Not all teenagers, though, think it's okay to kill in order to look good, be down or fit in. Not all teenagers think it's okay to kill for a pair of sneakers or a STARTER jacket. Those of you who would kill for clothes have your priorities all out of wack. The life that you and anybody else on the planet Earth live is worth far more than a STARTER jacket. Unfortunately, some kids aren't aware of this.

I respect the value of life.

March 3

I'm blessed, and I take full advantage of what I'm
blessed with.
—Deion Sanders

What are you blessed with? Do you like to draw? Is
it easy for you to make other people laugh? Are you
the one everyone in the class says would make a
good class president? Do you control the court the
minute you step on it? Make no mistake about it, the
Creator has given you something special. It's up to
you to discover what your gifts are and to begin using
them. For some of you, this may be hard. Why?
Because some of you have been told you're no good,
you're bad or you're stupid. If you believe those lies,
you probably haven't yet realized how special you
are. But make no mistake about it—you are *the* man!
You are *miss thing!* And each of you has stuff you
can work. Everybody has something special to give
to the world. Discover how special you are and what
special talents you possess.

*I take full advantage of what my Creator has blessed
me with.*

March 4

This business of who is more Hispanic than who—I call it passing the Hispanic test. It's ridiculous.
—Antonia Hernandez

Of course Puerto Ricans have a different culture than Mexicans who aren't just like Cubans who aren't exactly like Dominicans who are different from Panamanians who aren't the same as Salvadorans. No, all Latinos are not alike. But just because someone comes from a different country than you or speaks differently than you or is lighter skinned than you or prefers to be called Hispanic instead of Latino or Chicano doesn't mean he or she is any better or any worse than you. Like Ms. Hernandez says, judging who's the most Hispanics *is ridiculous* It's wack! Everyone has to learn how to learn from each other. Everyone has to learn that different does not mean worse. Different also doesn't mean better. Different is just different. Everybody and every culture are adding something wonderful and special to the world. We cannot let our differences divide us.

Instead of judging people, I see the beauty in differences.

March 5

I think it's a gross generality to think that all black people think alike and feel alike, just as it is to think all white people do.
—Debbye Turner

"Umph! She doesn't act black." "He's a wannabe." "Ooh, you're playing soccer, that's a white sport." "Oreo!" *Stop!* Who are you to tell another black person what black is? Some blacks grow up in neighborhoods where most of the families on the street are white. Some blacks grow up in predominantly black neighborhoods, and others grow up in mixed neighborhoods. Some blacks have parents who have white friends and friends from other cultures. Other blacks never see their parents socializing with anybody but black people. Some blacks grow up around other blacks who use slang. Other blacks grow up around whites who use a different slang and talk differently. Some blacks love to play soccer. Others have never tried the sport and don't really know whether or not they would or wouldn't like it *if* they tried it! Get the picture...

Each day I am more understanding, and I judge others less.

March 6

I've come from the worst, and I've been pulled down, but I'm here.
—Sharron Corley

As long as you're alive, you have a chance to make things better or worse for yourself. "But, why would I want to make my life worse?" You might not consciously set out to make things worse, but something called your unconscious mind sometimes contains negative, painful thoughts. Those thoughts control your actions whether or not you're aware of it. "But why would I wish bad for myself?" If you grow up in bad circumstances and that's what you're used to, then the unconscious part of you will want that to continue even though it's bad. "Why?" Because that's how your unconscious mind works. It sticks with what it knows, good or bad. How can you change your unconscious thinking? Through affirmations and prayer like you've already been doing! Remember, the power that gave you life wants you to be happy and prosperous, not sad and struggling.

My life is getting better and better all the time.

March 7

If you shoot for the stars and hit the moon, it's okay. But you've got to shoot for something. A lot of people don't even shoot.
—Robert Townsend

The power that created you wants you to be happy and prosperous. It wants you to fulfill your mission in life. You'll never fulfill your mission though unless you set some goals! Once you've set them, you've got to see them with your eyes closed. Once your mind is focused on your goals, your body will carry out the mind's intentions. If you challenged a blindfolded Michael Jordan to a free-throw shooting contest, do you think you'd win? Think about it. You can see the goal and he can't. Or can he! When you really believe in yourself, and when you can see a target with your eyes closed, you'll hit the target. *Remember, Michael did hit a free throw in an NBA game with his eyes closed!* Spend time thinking about your goals and seeing yourself successfully reaching them. It's like this: once you've seen it, you start to feel it. The next thing you know—nothing but net!

I see my future and it is wonderful!

March 8

And if a frog had wings, it wouldn't bump its ass.
—Mama Roxie

I wouldn't stop complaining one afternoon, so my grandmother, Mama Roxie, looked me dead in the eye and said, "And if a frog had wings, it wouldn't bump its ass." She didn't have to say another word because I immediately understood her point. *A frog will never have wings.* But unlike us humans, who complain about things we can't change, the frog just rolls with it. Many of you know or have known people like Mama Roxie. Our grandmothers and grandfathers have mad knowledge to share with us. When they speak, you'd be smart to pay close attention. Even if you can't get with what they're saying now, you'll be surprised at how when you're grown, married or in college, their words will come back to you and help you. You'll be like, "Word, my grandmother tried to tell me that back in the day."

I learn from those who are older and wiser than me.

March 9

The black kids, the poor white kids, Spanish-speaking kids, and Asian kids in the U.S.—in the face of everything to the contrary, they still bop and bump, shout and go to school somehow.
—Maya Angelou

Maya Angelou is talking about you. You didn't give up when things got rough. You worked hard, did what you had to do and got the job done. You graduated from grammar school and went on to middle and high school. You won spelling bees, track meets, state championships, school elections and scholarship money. You worked a part-time job and still made *A's* and *B's*. You got pregnant, had a baby and didn't drop out of school. You overcame peer pressure and didn't go along with the crowd. You helped your parents by taking care of your younger brothers and sisters while your parents worked. You pulled your grades up from D's and *F's* to *C's* and *B's*. In spite of the obstacles you've faced in life, you haven't give up or given in. Stand up and cheer for yourself. You deserve a standing ovation.

I get things done. I am somebody!

March 10

Ignorance has never been bliss. If we think education is expensive, try ignorance.
—Jocelyn Elders

Bliss is a state of complete happiness, and there's an old saying you may not have heard that goes, "Ignorance is bliss." It's similar to the one that says, what you don't know won't hurt you. Well, if you believe what you don't know won't hurt you and being ignorant is wonderful, then put down this book. Kids who read this book aren't interested in ignorance. They're interested in enlightenment. All of us are ignorant about some things. But being ignorant isn't the same as being stupid. When you're ignorant of something you need to know more about, you're smart if you find out about it. You're stupid if you don't. All of us are ignorant about those things we've never studied or been exposed to. But it's only those of us who choose not to educate, enlighten and inform ourselves who are stupid.

Knowledge is power. I am knowledgeable therefore I am powerful.

March 11

I was around people who were no good for me. I had to clean house, heal past wounds and concentrate on my soul.

—Dianne Reeves

Your soul, also called your spirit, is that part of you that never dies. Your spirit is that part of you that guides you and protects you, if you allow it to. Do you have a loving spirit? A mean spirit? A forgiving spirit? We're all born with loving spirits. Sometimes, though, fear comes along and causes us to get angry and start acting mean and hateful. When you concentrate on making your spirit loving and forgiving, you will want to be around others who are loving and forgiving. And you will begin to attract into your life people who are also loving and forgiving. When you decide to change your spirit, you may find yourself leaving some of your old friends behind. But that doesn't mean you stop loving those friends, just that you're moving on to a different life for yourself.

I attract people who are warm and loving because I am warm and loving.

March 12

> I had to cut everybody out of my camp. Every single person. I had to shake everybody and surround myself with the people that were focused on the same goals I had.
>
> —DJ Quik

Sometimes, changing your life means changing your environment. And sometimes, your environment is the people you hang with. It's normal for you to want to belong to a group. It's normal for you to want to be with the homies, the girls, your crew, your posse. And it's normal for you to want to be accepted by them. To get accepted you'll do things that you think will make them accept you. It's called peer pressure. Peer pressure is probably the hardest pressure you'll face in life. But if you want a future for yourself, you'll learn how to deal with peer pressure. You'll learn just like DJ Quik did. If you're hanging with the wrong crowd, you'll end up in the wrong place. If you're hanging with the right crowd, you'll end up in the right place. Period.

I hang with people who are doing the right things.

March 13

Your environment is what molds you.
—Lauryn Hill of the Fugees

Each of you is different because you each grow up in different environments. Do you wonder why you or some of your classmates crave attention? It's probably because you're not getting enough attention at home. Do you wonder why you or some of your classmates constantly get into fights? You're probably carrying around anger for something or someone, and unfortunately, you've learned that fighting is a way to express anger. It's easy to dog out people who act up and act out, but remember, people act according to how they've been brought up and what they've been through. If you don't like some things about yourself, work to change them. If you don't like some things about someone else, give them a break. As you mature, you'll learn to accept people as they are. You'll learn to accept both the good and the not-so-good parts of another person's personality.

I accept people as they are not as I want them to be.

March 14

I can't change anybody but myself, so I have to be a better me.
—Bill Duke

No matter how hard you try, you can never make anyone else act the way you want them to. Everybody has a brother or sister or classmate who drives them crazy. Each of you can name at least three things you'd like to change about someone else. Well, since you can't change even one thing about another person, why not change you? First, you have to be willing to change. Start by repeating this affirmation: "I am willing to change." And remember, change is often hard and seldom easy. But being willing to change opens up the door for change. The next step in the process of changing might mean talking over your problems with a licensed therapist or counselor, going into a drug or alcohol rehabilitation program, getting a part-time job to earn money instead of selling drugs or working harder in school to bring your grades up. The changing is on you.

I am willing to change.

March 15

I ain't perfect, but I want to be the best role model I can be.

—Montell Jordan

Read the next sentence carefully. *Nobody is perfect!* Everybody screws up, a lot, in life. Nobody is supposed to do everything perfectly. We're not supposed to be "angels." We're supposed to make mistakes, and perhaps make them again, but ultimately, we're supposed to learn from our mistakes. Kids who grow up thinking they have to be perfect are in for miserable lives. Why? Because when you want things to be perfect and they're not, you get angry and you do all kinds of crazy things. And when you think you have to be perfect and you mess up, you give yourself all kinds of hell—you beat yourself up. When you beat yourself up, you're not giving yourself a chance to grow and to change. Don't be so hard on yourself. You will never do everything perfectly. And other people will never be perfect for you. Ease up! Nothing and no one is perfect.

I'm not perfect and that's perfectly okay!

March 16

For as he thinks within himself, so he is.
—Proverbs 23:7

Have you ever walked into a store and gotten a funny look from the clerk behind the counter? Every day, you interact with strangers and sometimes those interactions are wack! Sometimes, people are mean or rude to you, and you feel dissed. Well, even though you may not see it, a salesclerk who is rude to you is probably rude to everyone—black folks, Latinos, white folks, Asians, everybody. Sometimes, other people's rudeness toward you has nothing to do with you or your skin color. Often, someone is having a bad day, and they take out their frustrations on whomever shows up. As you mature and become secure in who you are, you'll become less and less upset when strangers act rudely toward you. Until then, try to remember that sometimes when people are being rude, their rudeness has nothing to do with you.

I am good enough. I am a secure person.

March 17

I like the fact that I've gone through life without striking another human being in anger. I'm proud of it.

—E. Lynn Harris

When you're angry or upset, you sometimes want to fight. But you can't go through life fighting. Fighting can lead to shooting and gunshots can kill. If you can understand what you're really angry at, you can work at taming your anger. Sometimes, you're really angry at your mother for something she did or didn't do or you're angry at your father for selling you a dream. What happens though is you keep your anger for your parents inside until someone accidentally bumps into you in the hallway at school. Then you take the anger that was already there and unleash it on a classmate. The next thing you know, you're suspended from school, or worse, someone takes out a razor and cuts you. Get control of your anger! Talk out your feelings with your parents, your cousins, your teachers if they'll listen. Don't end up dead because you couldn't control your anger.

I express my anger in healthy, appropriate ways.

March 18

We start as fools and become wise through experience.
—Tanzanian proverb

You know a lot more now than you did when you were 3 years old. Why? Because of the lessons you've learned and the experiences you've had. The thing to remember about being a teenager is that you'll have many more experiences and learn many more lessons between now and the time you become a mature adult. Your experiences help you become a mature adult. Most of the time, you recognize positive experiences and that's cool. But sometimes, you have problems spotting negative experiences. Like when you don't realize that being high from drugs or alcohol, even though the high feels good, is *not* a positive experience. Think about it. When you're high, you don't think straight, and you don't drive straight either! And driving when you've been drinking or using drugs can kill you. If you don't learn from your negative experiences, you'll continue to repeat them with the same or worse results.

I learn my lessons so I don't have to repeat them.

March 19

Kids wanna get in the cars so they can visit girls, chill with other kids. There's a real innocence to the whole thing. Unless of course you're the one getting jackked.

—Nick Gomez

It's no fun having a gun or a knife put in your face by someone who's demanding that you get out of your car so they can drive off with it. Teens who car jack others, mug others or burglarize others' homes are forgetting the spiritual law that says what you put out, you get back. So are the teens who go to a friend's house for a party and then get drunk and trash the house. Word! For every action, there is a consequence. Sometimes the consequences come immediately, other times not. But don't be fooled. Even if you're never arrested for a crime you commit, even if you never serve jail time and even if you're not punished by your parents, you will still pay for your wrongdoing. What goes around, comes around.

I treat others the way I want to be treated.

March 20

Like most men, I used to define myself by external success. That's how we're taught to define ourselves. But real security comes from the inside.
—Laurence Fishburne

Society has many definitions for success. Have you ever fantasized about being onstage and having everybody in the audience going crazy over you? Is that success? Sometimes, when you fantasize about being on stage and being the center of attention, you're really fantasizing about being loved. Everybody wants to be loved. But being loved and feeling secure is not the same as being famous or successful. You can't put the screams of 16,000 fans in a bottle and drink it and get your love for the day. You may feel love when you're onstage with thousands of people screaming for you, but if you don't love yourself, once the concert ends, so does your feeling of being loved. There's nothing wrong with achieving success. But you'll never have true success or real security if you have to go outside yourself to find it. Real security comes from inside.

I am successful because I understand that love and security come from within.

March 21

Time has passed and the wounds have healed, and
I've moved on to other things.
—Keenen Ivory Wayans

Spring is a season of new beginnings. The power that
created our universe set it up that way. Spring
follows winter because in winter things die but are
replaced by new life in the spring. In nature, most
animals mate during the fall so that they bear their
offspring during spring when there is a greater
chance for the offspring to survive. Every day we
awaken is like spring. Each day is a new beginning
and a chance for us to do things differently and see
things differently. Take advantage of each new day
by letting go of yesterday's anger, hurt and
resentment. Holding on to anger and resentment for
others after they've hurt us is natural. But there comes
a time when not forgiving people is destructive. Old
anger and old hurts kept inside stress you out and
make you sick. Like Keenen says, wounds do heal,
and once they've healed, it's time to forgive and move
on.

*It is easy for me to let go of things that are no good
for me.*

March 22

Sometimes you're in the wrong place at the wrong time, or in a place you want to be but somebody else doesn't want you there and makes trouble for you.
—Dalvin of Jodeci

Do you sometimes feel as if trouble has a way of finding you? Well stop thinking and feeling that way! If you don't want trouble to find you, don't show up in those places where trouble might be lurking, waiting, hiding. You know, places like parties at three in the morning when your parents told you to be home by one. And places like the park across the street where fights break out and kids who are known troublemakers hang out. There are lots of things you can do to make it hard for trouble to catch up with you. Things like taking advice from friends, teachers and parents when they're trying to help you stay out of trouble. Things like listening to your inner voice, your gut feeling, your intuition when it's telling you not to go along with the crowd and give in to peer pressure. It may not be the easiest thing to do, but you can avoid trouble if you work at it.

I bring good situations into my life.

March 23

I grew up, couldn't read or write, so football gave me my personality. Once football was over, I had nothing to live for.

—Dexter Manley

Football, basketball, cars, money, women, men. What do all of these things have in common? None of them, let me repeat, none of them, is permanent. And none of them can give you a lasting sense of self-worth or value. Dexter Manley and many celebrities know this firsthand. Your sense of self-worth needs to come from inside you. Otherwise, once you're no longer a basketball or football hero or once you're no longer the world's top fashion model, or top singer, you feel empty inside. Don't get tricked into thinking that money, fame or a boyfriend or girlfriend makes you somebody special. You're special without those things, and if you have them, you were special before you got them. The love inside you makes you special. When you love you, you can grow up, become an NFL star, leave the NFL and still be a star because your life won't end just because your career did.

My self-worth comes from who I am on the inside.

March 24

I came to realize that if people could make me angry, they could control me. Why should I give someone else such power over my life?
—Ben Carson

"I did it because he made me mad." "She kept picking at me until I couldn't take it anymore." Sound familiar? Well, people are always going to do things you don't like. That's on them. How you react is on you. When you let someone else's actions control your reactions, you're giving your power away. What power? The power you have over your emotions. Others don't make you angry. You choose to get angry in reaction to something someone does. There's nothing wrong with getting angry. It's only when you blow up and express anger in negative ways that you give your power away. When you hold on to anger, that's even worse. Anger held inside can eat away at your insides and cause you to get sick. Learn how to express your anger without using violence or picking up a gun and shooting everybody. And learn to forgive once you've expressed your anger.

I am in control of my anger.

March 25

For minorities, sometimes the only way to assert their identity, to feel good about themselves, is to turn to another minority and say, 'You're not as good as us.'
—Forest Whitaker

When you don't feel good about who you are, you may try to put down someone else thinking you'll feel better if you do. Well, it doesn't work. It doesn't work for white people when they try to do it against minorities, and it won't work for you against another minority. Each so-called "race" has things it can be proud of and it's great to acknowledge those things. It's also okay to celebrate the first black or the first Latino or the first Asian to accomplish something great, but only if you remember that African-Americans, Hispanics and Asians have always had the ability to be great, even though they haven't always had the same opportunities as others! Now that you have more opportunities than your parents and grandparents did, are you going to sit around and dog out other minorities or are you going to begin acting like the wonderful person you are?

I feel good about who I am, and I have no need to put others down.

March 26

We all share life and that's a large enough common bond for us to try to live together.
—Cree Summer

We all breathe the same air. You've heard that before. But did you also know that we are all connected by the same energy—the energy that flows through the universe? The energy that flows through each of us? No matter what color or complexion we are, ebony, brown, ivory, sepia, honey-brown, pink, caramel, jet-black, pale, light, tanned, red-boned, butterscotch, yellow or white, we're all made up of the same stuff on the inside. None of us is better than the rest of us. Sure, some of us do some things better than others. But we're all talented. We've just been given different talents. No one can do what you do the way you do it! You are special. But so is Kyesha, Chilaun, Reggie, Kristen, Maria, Juan, Hyman, Chen, Julie, Stephanie, Rontae, Damon, John, Sheniqua, Dhan, Meng, Pedro, Bobby, Hong, Tamika, Sarah, Julio, Jason, James, Tanisha, Tamara and everybody else.

Everybody is special, and everybody deserves to be loved!

March 27

It's always a question of accepting responsibility for your choices. Anytime you look outside yourself for answers, you're looking in the wrong place.
—Oprah Winfrey

As long as you blame your parents, your friends, anybody but yourself for what happens in your life, you won't be able to change your life. Your friends may have lied on you to get you in trouble. If you have friends who are dishonest, maybe it's time to choose new friends. It may be true that you have parents who themselves aren't doing the right things. But using your parents' bad behavior as an excuse for your bad behavior doesn't make things any better for you. Every day, *you choose* to act good or bad. You choose to feel happy or sad, to act smart or dumb. If you're unhappy with the outcomes of your choices, it's time to make different choices. Remember, you have a purpose in life. You came to the planet Earth to make a contribution and to learn lessons. Don't let anyone, your parents, your friends or yourself stand in your way!

I take full responsibility for the choices I make.

March 28

You know what? Racism is a given. You could spend the rest of your life trying to figure out who's racist and who's not. So what, who cares? Get busy wit' yourself.

—Denzel Washington

When you decide to take control of your own destiny, racism is not a problem for you. Why? Because when you decide how you want your life to be, you let nothing and no one stop you from making it so! Racism is not an obstacle, it's just another challenge you overcome and kick to the curb. Racism is not the excuse you give when someone asks you why you're selling drugs, or why you're not doing well in school. Of course racism exists. But is it really racism that's keeping you from dreaming? No. It's your anger about racism and discrimination that's holding you back. It's normal to be angry about racism. It would be great if *everybody* in America were angry about racism. It would be even better if everybody would turn their anger into activism and work to get rid of racism. *You've got to turn your anger to activism!* Meet racism head on and overcome it. Now get busy!

Racism has no power over me.

March 29

Standing up and calling everybody a whole bunch of motherfuckers is not the same as controlling your destiny.

—Melvin Van Peebles

You can control your destiny! But like Mr. Van Peebles says, cursing and getting in people's faces is *not* the way to have a life destined for good things. Kids who curse and fight may think they have things under control, but they don't. They curse and fight to try to regain the control they think they've lost. But if you have to curse and fight, you were never really in control. Afterward, things are no better than before. Everyone needs to understand they can't control other people. But you can control you. You can control your destiny! The way you control your destiny is by deciding where you want to go in life and figuring out the best way to get there. And remember, the best way may not be the easiest way. Once you know where you're going and how best to get there, you can stop all your cursing and do whatever it takes to allow your destiny to unfold.

I am in control of my destiny.

March 30

At all the critical junctures in my life, there seemed to be a teacher around to guide me.
—Jimmy Smits

Question: Are all African-Americans good at sports?
Answer: No.
Question: Are all Puerto Ricans on welfare?
Answer: No.
Question: Are all teachers bad?
Answer: No.

You've met teachers who tried to help you tap into your unlimited potential. Did you accept their help? Remember, there are good teachers and there are bad teachers, just as there are students who act right in class and students who don't. It's time to stop lumping everybody into one broad category and stereotyping them for life. When you meet teachers who try to help you become your best, accept their help! And remember them the next time you start doggin' out all teachers.

I am willing to accept help when it is offered to me.

March 31

If you have an opportunity to make things better and you don't do that, you're wasting your time on this earth.

—Roberto Clemente

In 1966, Roberto Clemente became the first Latino to be named professional baseball's most valuable player. In 1972, Clemente, a Puerto Rican, died in a plane crash. He wasn't on his way to a game. He wasn't going on vacation. Clemente was part of a relief team flying to Nicaragua to take food and medicine to people left homeless by an earthquake. In his few years on earth, Clemente helped make things better. Learn a lesson from him. Begin in your own home. If you live in a troubled home, get help for yourself. Professional therapists can help you understand what's going on around you so it doesn't beat you down and destroy you. Then, you can reach out to others. You can volunteer at a homeless shelter. You can get involved in your student government association. You *can* make the world a better place.

I am helping to make the world a better place.

April 1

The practice of self-love is something that we must be vigilant about.
                    —bell hooks

I love and approve of myself. My higher power loves and approves of me. I believe in a power far greater than I am that created me and lives inside me. I am one with the power that created me, and that power has given me the power to create my own destiny. I believe in myself! I am good enough! I am no longer afraid of things, and I no longer accept the limitations others try to put on me. I am no longer stressed by the fears or the prejudices of society. Things are going to work out for me! I am a good person and I deserve to have good things happen to me. I am patient and understanding and forgiving. I am willing to change the way I think about myself and other people. And I trust my inner wisdom to guide me. I respect myself and so do others. Love surrounds me and protects me. Others love me because I love me.

I am loving and lovable and loved!

April 2

Better to try than not to try at all.
—Selena

Teachers, parents and counselors who care about you are tired of hearing "I don't know," and "I don't care" from you. Some of you have made a career out of saying you don't know or you don't care to people trying to teach you and help you. It's too soon for you to stop trying in school. It's too early in the game for you to decide you no longer care. When you say you don't care, I say, bull! You really do care, it's just that you're so afraid to try. So you take the easy way out by saying you don't care and giving up. The good news about being teenagers is that you're not expected to struggle alone. Parents, teachers and counselors want to help you with whatever it is you're struggling with. But you have to be willing to accept help. You have to be courageous enough to care.

I care about what happens to me.

April 3

Whatever situation you find yourself in, you must work hard to do your best and make no excuses.
—Ayinde Jean-Baptiste

Ask anybody who's successful in life whether they worked hard to get where they are. Most of them will tell you they worked very hard. They might even tell you that nothing really worth having comes easily. Some of you are quite familiar with hard work. Your hard work earned you a place in your school's Honor Society, a first-place finish in an essay contest or a promotion on your part-time job. Others of you have decided you don't want to work hard. Maybe you've seen your parents struggle or heard them talk about how hard they work, and you formed a negative attitude about hard work. Well, remember this: few things really worth having in life come easily. So you either sign up for the best life has to offer and you work hard to get those things, or you take the easy way out and settle for garbage.

I achieve my goals because I work hard.

April 4

Everybody can be great. Because anybody can serve.
You don't have to have a college degree to serve.
　　　　　—Dr. Martin Luther King, Jr.

If you decide you don't need a college education to
help you fulfill your life's mission, that doesn't mean
you're not as valuable as someone who chooses to go
to college. Oseola McCarty quit school in the sixth
grade because her aunt became sick. She began
working full-time, washing and ironing clothes, so
she could support her aunt and grandmother. She had
dreamed of going to college to become a nurse, but
Miss Oseola never went back to school. She spent
the next 75 years washing and ironing clothes. In
1995, at age 87, Miss Oseola donated more than half
of her life's savings, $150,000, to the University of
Southern Mississippi for scholarships for blacks.
One hundred fifty thousand beans! Word! You don't
find greatness or success inside a college. You find it
in you. And once you find it, you'll know just like
Miss Oseola did that you can serve and be great even
if you never set foot in anybody's college!

The road to greatness begins inside me.

April 5

Affirmative action is a moot point if you don't learn to read and write.
—Jesse Jackson

Although approximately 25 percent of girls and 8 percent of boys drop out of high school when they become parents, many more dropouts say they drop out because they're bored with school and they just don't like it. If you're thinking about leaving school because you don't like it, think again. When you choose not to become educated, you limit your career choices. How many of you know kids or adults who regret that they didn't get an education when they had the chance? If you've already dropped out of school, you may be having second thoughts. Whether you leave school early or walk across the stage with your diploma in hand, you've got to be educated if you're going to make it in the world. Some of you graduate without having obtained a good education. If that's the case, you're probably no better prepared than the person who has no diploma.

My education is important to me.

April 6

I don't think that half the stuff on the radio now really needs to be heard. I mean, how much more can you hear about sex, violence and guns.
—Malik Yoba

How many times can you listen to someone sing about you in a way that puts you down? In a way that demeans and devalues you? To answer that last question, you might ask yourself just how much are you worth? How much do you mean to you? Once you've answered those questions, you can then decide how much to put up with. Words, images and ideas that are negative can only have negative effects. There's a saying you may not have heard—garbage in, garbage out. Feed your mind with negative images and ideas, and soon, you'll be acting out those negative images and ideas. Feed your mind with positive images and ideas and you'll develop a positive self-image and do positive things. Hopefully, when you get tired of hearing songs and watching videos that put you down and demean you, you'll stop listening and watching.

I am surrounded with images and ideas that uplift me.

April 7

To be a champion, you have to believe in yourself when nobody else will.
—Sugar Ray Robinson

Many teens spend a lot of time trying to prove themselves to others. If you're Hispanic or black, your parents may have told you you have to be twice as good and work twice as hard as whites to make it in life. Your parents are right in understanding that minorities are discriminated against and treated unfairly by some in the majority. But even though you may have to work harder to achieve the same things as others, that doesn't make them any better than you. Whenever you're trying to prove something to someone, ask yourself why. If you're trying to prove something you already know, something like, "I'm smart and I can achieve whatever I want in life," great! But if you feel like you're not as good as someone else and you think you need to prove you are—stop! You are as good as anybody else! Believe it!

I believe in myself. I am good enough!

April 8

I knew I had to do it.
—Kerri Strug, Olympic Gold Medalist

YES

YOU

CAN!

Yes, I Can!

April 9

You always have to have something to depend on or fall back on. No one can take your education away from you.
—Monica

There are some things in life you should never give up. You should never sacrifice your principles and you should never let anyone steal your soul. And, like Monica says, your education is something that, once you own it, no one can take it away from you. Oh sure people will try to tell you you're dumb or stupid. People may tell you you're wrong, and you don't know what you're talking about. Don't stress that. You know how smart you are. You've studied and worked hard, and you know what's true and what isn't. Because you've read and studied and gained knowledge beyond what you've been taught in school, you're ready to make your mark in the world. You're ready to take your education and make it work for you.

No one can take my education away from me.

April 10

If you plant turnips, you will not harvest grapes.
—Akan Proverb

The Akan are a tribal people who live in Ghana, Ivory Coast and parts of Togo, countries on the African continent. And they understand spiritual laws. There is a spiritual law of cause and effect. It means simply, what you put out, you get back. If you constantly think bad, mean, hateful thoughts, then you'll do bad, mean, hateful things. And if you do bad things, bad will come back to you. There are many bad things happening in our world now, and many of them are out of your control. But you can control your mind. Don't be afraid of getting shot if you live in a neighborhood where there is shooting all the time or if there's been a shooting at your school. Begin planning your future in your mind. See yourself growing up, getting a job or going to college or trade school. Think only about those things you want to happen in your life. If you want grapes, then plant grapes—in your mind!

Whatever I think about, I become.

April 11

If we don't take good care of our body, where will we live?

—Anonymous

You ain't getting another body so it would be smart to take care of the one you have. Remember that saying "garbage in, garbage out?" If you put bad things into your body, your body will put out bad things—things like aches and pains and illnesses. If you remember that your body is the house for your soul, you might start taking better care of the house. On a piece of paper, write down all the things you do that are good for your body. Now write down all the things you do that are bad for your body. Now, write down three things you know are good for your body that you don't do. If you want to make some changes, do this: Pick one thing from your list of all the things you do that are bad for your body, and stop doing it! Then, pick one of the three things you're not doing that would be good for your body and start doing it! Remember, you only get one body.

I have a healthy body because I treat it right.

April 12

By trying often the monkey learns to jump from the tree.

—Cameroon Proverb

Have you tried to meditate? Was it easy? Hard? If you stopped, how long did you stick with it? Well, let's try again. This time, lets stick with it for 30 days! If you do something for 30 days straight, it often becomes a habit and you can keep doing it for a long time. The purpose of meditating is to connect with your spiritual self. Remember, your spirit is that part of you that gives you life and that never dies. When you sit quietly, with your back straight and your eyes closed and you concentrate on a sound and ignore your thoughts, you're meditating. If you find yourself paying attention to your thoughts, just go back to concentrating on your breathing. The key to mastering anything in life is keep at it. And you'll see that in 30 days, you've begun to spend more time listening to your breathing and less time paying attention to your many thoughts.

I meditate regularly so I can connect with my spirit.

April 13

The nightmare ends when you say it does.
>   —Dr. Cushing in *Tales From the Hood*

Are you in a bad situation that seems to be getting worse? Do you sometimes think, "I hate my life?" Listen up: until you decide to get rid of the things that have you all stressed out, those things will stay with you. The nightmare ends when you say so! It's called problem solving. In order to solve a problem, you've got to first recognize that you have a problem. If you're angry a lot or depressed a lot, you have a problem. And there's a reason for your anger or your depression. Talking things over with a licensed therapist or counselor can help you understand why you're angry or depressed. And that's the second step in problem solving—understanding why you have the problem. The third step is finding a solution. It may take some time for you to solve your problems, but you'll never solve them until you face up to them. The nightmare ends when you say so!

I am smart enough to know when I've got problems, and I choose the best ways to get rid of my problems.

April 14

There's nothing wrong with 'do unto others as you would like others to do unto you.'
—Andy Garcia

Do unto others as you would have them do unto you. How many times has your father or mother or the person taking care of you said that to you? What about, "So if all the other kids are going to jump off a bridge, you'll jump off it too?" Or, "Two wrongs don't make a right." Why do you think your parents say these things over and over? Do you think it's because they don't like you and they want you to have a messed-up life? Or do you think they say these things because they love you and are trying to teach you something important? The next time you hear your parents say something you've heard a million times before, why not stop and think about what it is they're really saying before you flip. If you really think about what they're saying, you may find you don't have any reason to flip. Doing unto others as you would have them do unto you will take you far in life. You don't think so? Try it and see.

I treat people with the same respect I want from them.

April 15

But I think parents should listen to their kids too.
—Brandy

Nobody knows everything. Not even parents! And there are probably times when you think your parents should listen to you, but they don't. They just yell and scream and they won't listen to your side of the story. That sucks. It makes you mad. You feel as though you're powerless and not in control of your life. Well, sometimes, your parents won't listen to you because they're afraid to hear what you're trying to tell them! They're afraid because they don't think they can handle what you're saying. And sometimes, they feel like they can't help you with whatever it is you need help with. Yeah, it would be great if your parents listened to you more—I mean really listened to you. But remember, parents make mistakes too. They're afraid to deal with things too sometimes.

I am more understanding when it comes to my parents.

April 16

I feel like this: nothing in this world is worth more than your happiness.
   —Nas

Everybody wants to find happiness, but many of us are looking in the wrong places. Happiness doesn't come from a store or from another person or from being famous. Your happiness can come only from inside you. The power that created you has equipped you with everything you need to be happy. But being happy doesn't mean you'll always have everything you want. And once you find happiness, that doesn't mean you'll never experience sadness. Being happy means you've learned to trust that everything is working together for your ultimate good. When you understand that your God has your back and God will support you in whatever you choose, you'll begin making smarter choices. Instead of choosing to be afraid all the time, you'll learn to believe that things will work out even though you can't possibly see how.

My happiness comes from inside me.

April 17

God gave us faces. We make our own expressions.
—Anonymous

Did you draw a happy face? A sad face? No face? Why don't you fill in the face now. Draw it however you're feeling. Now, remember, you're in control of your happiness—not your parents, not your friends, not some stranger, not your boyfriend or girlfriend— *you!* Sure people can do things to cause you grief, but you're still choosing grief, you're choosing to be upset. You can put on a happy face any time you choose, and you can put on a sad face any time you choose. Of course no one is happy all the time. But there are times when you choose to stress things you could just as easily forget. Learn to see the good life has to offer instead of constantly seeing bad. Choose a happy face!

I choose to be happy.

April 18

All the problems you experience in the world are right here in jail.
—Slick Rick

Being locked up is no picnic. Some kids think it's no big deal to be sent to juvenile detention. Some kids think it's fun to be locked up if their friends are also locked up. Wrong! Just ask Slick Rick. Whatever was going on with you on the outside will be with you when you're locked up. And having your friends there is not going to make things any better. The smart thing to do is to avoid those situations that lead to getting arrested and locked up in the first place. Because no matter what some of you tell yourselves, you were *not* born to be a thug! You were *not* born bad! Some of you do things that are wrong and you think you won't get caught. Wrong again! All of your actions have consequences. If you break the law and you get caught, there are consequences. If you break the law and don't get caught, there are still consequences. Remember that.

I make smart choices that keep me on the right side of the law.

April 19

Friendship has to be based on trust.
—Camille Cosby

Do you have friends you trust and who trust you? Do you have true friends who will stick with you no matter what? Sometimes, we think people are our friends when they're really not. Sometimes, we join clubs, groups or gangs because we're looking for friendship and love. But can you really find true friends and trust in a gang? Can people who are doing wrong things really be trusted? If you're in a gang and your gang is about something positive, great! But if you're running with a gang that's involved in drugs and violence and payback, ask yourself, "How much can I really trust the people I'm running with?" When bullets start flying, where are your friends? When you're picked up by the police, are your homies there with you? Ask yourself this: are your fellow gang members friends or just accomplices? Are they friends or just crime partners?

I have friends who are trustworthy.

April 20

Don't catch an attitude with me!
> —Warning from someone
> who's not having it!

What's your attitude like? Do you usually have a good attitude? A bad attitude? An optimistic attitude? As a teenager, you'll try out many attitudes. That's because teenagers undergo lots of changes as you try to figure out what life is all about. It's normal for you to go through changes, and it's normal for you to try out different attitudes. But if you go though life with a nasty attitude, no one will want to be around you. People often have nasty attitudes because they're holding on to anger and won't let it go. Anger is a powerful feeling, but, just like anything else, anger can be controlled. If anger can't seem to leave you alone, you've got to find out what's got you so angry. Then, you've got to find a way to let go of your anger.

I let go of the anger that's behind my nasty attitude.

April 21

The people who take care of you and make sure you have food on the table and a roof over your head are the ones you should look up to.
—Ken Griffey Jr.

Some teens' thoughts when asked to say the first thing that comes to mind when they hear the word *parents:* Part of your life. Role models. Teachers. Providers. Rules. A friend. Chilren. Good. Mean. Instructing. Love. Loving. Friendship. Strict. Overprotective. Someone you should be able to look up to. Bosses. Somebody that's there for you all the time. Hard to talk to. Supposed to love you. Creator—well being. Supposed to be there for you. Nag. Overseers. Somebody to kiss your boo-boos. Sometimes they're friends.

I appreciate the good things my parents do for me.

April 22

When your mother and father talk to you, you should listen. Sometimes you get mad at them. That's natural. But you should be grateful to them, because a united family is the basic foundation for having a good chance at life.
—Juan Gonzalez

If you have parents who take care of you financially, support you emotionally and encourage you to be your best, count your blessings! Some kids aren't as lucky as you. And even though your parents get on your nerves, try not to shut them out. They understand you're a teenager who's trying to figure out who you are. They understand you're trying to assert your independence and you have a need to break away from them. But you have to understand that they want the best for you, and they naturally want to protect you. They know what's out there, and when they start nagging you, they're only trying to help you stay out of trouble and away from bad situations. Ease up on your parents. If you want them to show you more respect and understanding, show them more respect and understanding.

I respect my parents.

April 23

A person who talks too much often let's life's lessons
slip by so I'd rather absorb.
—Gerald Levert

Sometimes, we forget how important it is to pay
attention when someone is trying to tell or teach us
something. Sometimes, we're so busy interrupting the
teacher because we want to get attention that we miss
out on valuable information. Other times, we're so
busy interrupting our parents or our friends that we
don't hear what they're trying to tell us. What we've
got to remember is no one knows everything there is
to know, and everyone has something more to learn.
And learning can be fun, if you allow it to be fun. If
you want to learn more about life, you have to be
willing to listen more. And you listen more when
you talk less.

I listen more and talk less.

April 24

When you do something bad, something good can come out of it.
—Jason Kidd

Have you ever been picked up by the police? Locked up? Sent to In School Suspension or been kicked out of school? If not, do you know someone who has? Well, getting in trouble is not the end of the world. Remember, doing bad and being a bad person are two different things. Doing bad things doesn't make you a bad person, just a person making bad choices. And getting into trouble as a teenager doesn't mean you're headed for a lifetime of trouble, unless that's what you want. It's never too late to turn things around. If you're doing oay but have friends who get into trouble, tell them not to give up on themselves, even if their parents, their teachers and everybody else has given up on them. If you're getting into trouble and it seems as though everyone has given up on you, you can't give up on you. If you do something bad, turn the bad thing into a good thing by learning from it and moving past it.

I learn lessons from bad situations.

April 25

Through my family's love, I now realize that it was not my fault that I was given away.
—Anita Baker

Kids who are adopted are just as special as kids who aren't given up for adoption. The problem comes when kids who are given away don't realize how special they are. You see, just because your parents gave you up for adoption doesn't mean there's something wrong with you. Everybody struggles at some point in their lives. And when we struggle, we get through our struggles the best way we know how. And if your parents gave you up for adoption, they were probably going through some serious struggles. The important thing to understand, though, is that there's nothing wrong with you if you are adopted. You're just as special as anybody else on the planet. There is nothing wrong with you just because you are adopted.

I am a good kid who deserves all the love I can get!

April 26

It's really terrible that there's so many people supposed to be normal who don't have the heart to be kind to people who are different.
—Loretta Claiborne

Loretta Claiborne was born retarded and legally blind. She didn't begin walking until age 4 after an eye operation helped her see better. Her eyes remained crossed, however, and Loretta got called "Clarence the Cross-Eyed Lion." Instead of putting her in an institution as she'd been advised, Loretta's mother kept her in special classes at the public school. But kids always wanted to beat Loretta up. Kids would walk behind Loretta and push her. At age 12, Loretta began running at night with her brother, Hank, a top state cross-country runner. In high school, Loretta ran in her first Special Olympics running competition. At age 27, she ran the Boston Marathon and placed in the top 100 women finishers. By 1995, 42-year-old Loretta Claiborne had completed 26 marathons, earned a black belt in karate, mastered sign language and learned to speak some Russian and Spanish.

I treat people who are different with respect and kindness.

April 27

You don't have to like the state you're in to still like yourself.
　　　　—BeBe Winans

Each of us has things we don't like about ourselves. But like BeBe says, it's okay if you don't like some things about yourself, as long as you don't stop liking you! If you've been trying to change some things you don't like about you, and if you've been saying your affirmations to help you change, cool! But remember, affirmations aren't magic! Don't think you're going to get a boyfriend by repeating 200 times "I have a wonderful boyfriend who treats me with respect," unless, deep down, you really believe you deserve to be treated with respect! Sometimes, deep down in your unconscious mind, you have negative, painful thoughts you need to get rid of. When you let go of these negative, painful thoughts, your affirmations can become real for you. And it's a lot easier to let go of painful thoughts and ideas when you begin to love yourself and accept yourself.

I am patiently learning how to love myself no matter what.

April 28

No matter what else happens in your life, no matter how many mistakes you make, there's always going to be a higher power there to accept and love you.
—Larry Pound

Your higher power lives inside you—always. You and your higher power cannot be separated. Sometimes, you may forget about your higher power. You may neglect your spiritual side, but your spiritual side is still there. Even when things seem to be all screwed up, your higher power is there. Even when you're confused, your higher power is still there. No, you won't always have all the answers, but you've got to understand that not having all the answers is okay. As you mature and get older, you'll understand more about yourself and about life. That's what maturing is all about. That's what growing up is all about. But isn't it great to know you don't have to go through life alone? Isn't it great to know you were born with a power great enough to see you through any situation or circumstance. No matter what you call your higher power, it's always there to accept and love you.

I trust my higher power to see me through.

April 29

I have a very close relationship with God.
—Kenny Blank

You *will* come to your own understanding of God. For some, God is like a person who lives in heaven. Others think of God as a force that doesn't have a shape or a body but is everywhere. They believe that this God-force, this creative force lives inside them and is part of them. Some think this force is the same force that creates love—the love that exists inside each of us. Others understand this creative force to be the same one that speaks to them—you know, that little voice inside you that speaks to you, not in words, but in a feeling. Some see it as the force that guides them. They think this force is always with them and will help them fulfill their mission in life. Some people call this force their higher power, others Spirit, still others call it their Creator or the Universe, and others, simply God. Some even think that each one of us is God in different disguises!

I am coming to my own understanding about God.

April 30

The past is over and the future is yet to be.
—Jerry Jamplosky

Today, you have an opportunity to write your own text and affirmation. Please begin by repeating "the past is over and the future is yet to be." Now, get some paper and a pen and write down what you think the phrase means for you. Write as much or as little as you want, then come up with an affirmation for yourself. When you're done, you can even write your affirmation at the bottom of this page if you like. Peace!

*I am*_____

In the beginning . . .

May 1

If you know whence you came, there is really no limit to where you can go.
—James Baldwin

The oldest fossils of man were found in Tanzania on the African continent. Some of the first civilized people, Nubians, also called Ethiopians, lived in Africa. But you're not taught the truth in schools about African history and the beginning of civilization. Textbooks tell you about the how Africans were enslaved. But African history doesn't begin with slavery. And African-Americans weren't enslaved because they were inferior to whites, even though that's what was said. To know where you come from, or in other words, to know your history, you can't just memorize what happened and when. You have to learn and understand the truth about *why* things happened. In this section, you will learn the truth. You'll also gain a better understanding of where you and others came from, and you'll begin to see just how far and how high you can go!

I know where I come from, and I'm proud of it!

May 2

A lot of people can't believe that we came from Africa.
—Edward James Olmos

Marriages between Spaniards, Africans and Arawak Indians—people who lived on an island near Cuba—created Puerto Ricans. Unions between Europeans, African and Indian people also created Latinos in Central and South America. Mexicans are primarily a mixture of Indians and Europeans. But even though you can be proud of your ancestry, understand that all of us can trace our origins to Africa, and we're all one race! Scientists understand there are no biological differences that prove human beings with different skin color belong to different races. And the notion that one so-called race is superior over another so-called race is wack. The power that created the universe didn't create us Negroid or Mongoloid or Caucasoid. We don't belong to separate races. Racial groups were made up by men and they keep people divided. The creator created the human race, and it's up to us to know that!

I am proud of my ancestry and happy that my Creator doesn't discriminate.

May 3

New stories had to be written; those of the white man
and the savage were not really my story.
—Chinua Achebe

Writers like Nigerian, Chinua Achebe, understand
how harmful it is to have your culture or your so-
called race negatively portrayed. That's why he
began writing stories about the Ibo, people who live
in northeastern Nigeria, a country on the continent of
Africa—the second largest continent in the world.
There are 52 countries in Africa, a continent more
than three times as large as the United States. The
people living in Africa, mainly blacks and Arabs with
a small number of whites and Asians, have been
portrayed negatively for far too long. Like Achebe
says, they've been portrayed as savages needing to be
rescued by whites. Whenever you read or hear
something about your history and your culture, don't
be so quick to believe it. Do your own investigating
and find out the truth.

I am a truth seeker.

May 4

We have to pull ourselves out of that intellectual lethargy that has made us believe we do not have sufficient brains to enter the field of science.
—Franklin R. Chang-Diaz

Costa Rican-born Franklin R. Chang-Diaz, is one of a handful of Latino astronauts. When he says Latinos can be scientists, he understands Latino history. He knows that the Mayans were scientists. Before being invaded by Spaniards, Mayans lived in southern Mexico and also Belize, Guatemala and Honduras. The Mayan Indians were expert mathematicians and astronomers. They began studying the sun, moon and stars so they could predict weather patterns and thus, know when to plant and harvest their crops. Mayans developed several calendars and were fascinated with time. They invented the concept of zero, which is today the basis of our numerical system. Mayans also built pyramids, just like the ancient Nubians and Egyptians built pyramids. Question: If your Mayan ancestors understood astronomy and math—why can't you? Answer: *you can!*

I can do mat, too! Science is for me!

May 5

Freedom. To keep it, you have to fight for it, and every generation has to win it over again.
—Cesar Chavez

On May 5, 1862, a small group of Mexican fighters defeated Napoleon's huge French army at the battle of Puebla. That's why in Mexico, Cinco de Mayo is a national holiday celebrated with a big military parade. In America, Cinco de Mayo is thought of as Mexican Independence Day even though it's really September 16. Long before they fought off the French, Mexicans had to gain their freedom from Spain who had ruled them for 300 years. On Sept. 16, 1810, Father Miguel Hidalgo y Costilla went into town and told his parishioners to revolt against Spain. Eleven years later, Mexico defeated Spain and gained control of its country. Beginning in the 1960s, Cesar Chavez, a Mexican migrant farm worker, began fighting by boycotting and protesting unfair working conditions. Word! Don't ever be afraid to stand up and fight for what you believe in.

I will stand up and fight for my beliefs.

May 6

A wise man who know proverbs reconciles difficulties.
> —Yoruba Proverb

Proverbs, like the one above and like others in this book, a are very important in African countries. Proverbs come from folk stories told by Africans and were often the last words spoken to sum up the story. They were considered to be what we in America call the moral of the story. Some groups in Africa even use proverbs to help them argue their legal cases. There are several American sayings that are similar to African proverbs. The American saying "the dogs bark is worse than his bite" resembles the African proverb, "the dog's bark is not might, but fright." All cultures have sayings or proverbs. There are Yiddish proverbs, Mexican sayings, Puerto Rican sayings, Native American proverbs, Hindu proverbs, Chinese proverbs and on and on. Why don't you do some research and discover some proverbs or sayings that are a part of your cultural heritage!

Each day, I learn more and more!

May 7

When I was introduced to African culture and realized that many people were trying to keep this knowledge away from me, I was driven to learn more and more about myself.
—Speech

For years, many historians denied Latinos and African-Americans their true place in world history and in American history. Many truths about them has been either ignored or altered. And even though several historians and writers have documented the truth, you're generally not reading their books in school. So now what? Now, you do what Speech did. You learn the truth. Too many people think African-American history begins with slavery. It doesn't. And all Latinos—Puerto Ricans, Chicanos, Panamanians, Dominicans, Salvadorans, Cubans, Mexicans and Mexican-Americans—have their own histories. So do the diverse group of people commonly called Asians, i.e. Japanese, Chinese, Filipinos to name a few. Don't sit around feeling angry because you're not being taught the truth. Go to your local libraries and read and learn the truth!

I am learning the truth about history.

May 8

It's easy to look at the negative side of things....But you know, I think there is always a positive outlook on something.

—Michael Chang

How can anyone possibly have a positive outlook on America's racial problems? Given America's history of racism against Asians, should Michael Chang, a Chinese-American, be expected to have a positive outlook? At the turn of the century, Asian immigrants couldn't own or lease land, and it was unlawful for them to testify against whites in court. During World War II, Japanese-Americans were forced into internment camps. Yes, the past was messed up for certain groups of people. But we've got to deal with the present! I know you think there are different races. Not! We're all part of *The Human Race*. The idea that we're different races based on our skin color is a lie that began in the 1700s. When you understand that labels like black, white, Native American, Asian and Latino don't mean what you've been taught, you'll understand that w*e can conquer racism.*

We are one planet, one race, many shapes, sizes and colors!

May 9

Look at individuals, not races.
　　　　　　　—Carlos Mencia

If you're Puerto Rican and you hear on the news that a woman out jogging was grabbed, raped and killed by two men, do you say to yourself, "I hope the guys who did it weren't Puerto Rican?" If you're African American, do you also hope the perpetrators don't belong to your race? If you answer yes, why? Because you think white people will say "See, there *they* go again." And you feel that when one member of your race messes up, it makes everybody look bad. Well, why do you care what white people think? And what makes whites think they can judge all blacks, Latinos and Asians by what one does? It's called "white superiority." It's the idea many whites have that they're superior. Unfortunately, many minorities also think whites are superior. No so-called "race" is superior. Carlos has it right. Look at individuals, not races.

I look at individuals, not races.

May 10

I was like 15 years old, Ma dukes couldn't dress a
nigga no more and at that age you want a little money
in your pocket. That's what gets us all, material
possessions.

—Kool G Rap

Centuries ago, Africans were enslaved by other
Africans and later, by Europeans who shipped them
to America and made them work for free. Europeans
made mad money off "slave" labor. The average age
of Africans captured and shipped abroad into slavery
was fourteen. Indians were also enslaved. Mayans
and the Arawak (also called Tainos) who lived in
what is now Mexico and Puerto Rico were enslaved
by Spaniards who came to their islands looking for
gold. They then robbed, murdered and enslaved the
Indians and took their gold and their land. Today,
some of us seem to think the only thing in life worth
having is gold—loot—money! We steal, sell drugs or
get others to sell drugs for us so we can make that
money. We've become slaves to money! Ask yourself
this, "Is my life only about money and clothes and
cars?"

My life is about more than material things.

May 11

It's up to us Afro-Americans to reclaim the grandeur of our heritage.

—Wynton Marsalis

For too long, African-Americans have been put down and told they're no good. But African-Americans have a lot to be proud of just like Asians, whites, Latinos and Native Americans have a lot to be proud of. African-Americans have a heritage that reaches back to Africa. In ancient African societies, women were queens and they were respected and revered. African women made perfume from oils. They made wigs to protect their heads from the sun. They used the plants and soil to create make-up. They rubbed indigo and copper on their eyes to protect their eyes from the sun's glare. African men wove beautiful clothes. African men and women wrote books, devised governmental systems, charted the stars, built pyramids, ruled their countries and defended their lands in battle. See how much you have to be proud of!

I'm proud of my heritage!

May 12

In Nigeria, if you show disrespect for anyone older than yourself, you are punished.
—Hakeem Olajuwon

Hakeem, a professional basketball player, is from Nigeria, an African country twice the size of California. More than 100 million people—the most of any African country—live in Nigeria. Hakeem grew up in Lagos, Nigeria where, as in many African societies, the entire community takes responsibility for raising children. And, as Hakeem says, disrespect for those older than you is not allowed. In America, we make a big deal about respect and disrespect. But what is respect and how do we get it? When someone respects you, they look up to you and they admire you. You get respect by doing the right things. You don't get respect by bullying people around. When you make people afraid of you, they may do what you want, but they won't respect you, they'll hate you! Please don't confuse fear with respect.

I understand the difference between fear and respect.

May 13

The days of us keeping each other down, the days of us fighting each other and not understanding there is tremendous power in unity are over.
—Arsenio Hall

There's an old African proverb that says, "A slave who knows how to serve succeeds to his master's property." Before the Europeans came to Africa looking for gold and later, "slaves," Africans in different countries, belonging to different tribes and clans enslaved other Africans. Why? Back then, in Africa, in Europe and throughout the world, prisoners of war were made to be slaves. Criminals were also deported to others countries and used as slaves. In African countries, slaves were not viewed as property, and, as the proverb indicates, they weren't treated badly like they were in America. But when Europeans came to Africa looking for slaves, Africans captured other Africans and traded them to the Europeans for iron, textiles, guns and gunpowder. Like Arsenio says, there is power in unity. But when we make war on each other and keep each other down, we set each other up for much worse things!

I make peace with all my brothers and sisters.

May 14

A friend of mine told me recently that when you feel your spirit being sucked dry, when you feel the spirit God gave you being taken away—that's when it's not right, and you have to let go.

—Whitney Houston

During the slave trade, many Africans were captured inland and walked to the coast to be sold. In Benin, a small west African country, the route the Africans walked was called the Road of Slaves. Along the Road of Slaves, the people who captured the Africans and chained them together made the men, women and children stop and walk around trees. They were told that because they walked around those trees, they had lost their spirits, they were no longer human and their lives no longer mattered. *They were lied to.* Today, it seems as though some of us have walked around some spirit-stealing trees. Some of us think we don't matter. *You do matter!* And like Whitney says, if you feel your spirit being sucked dry or if someone is telling you you don't matter—get as far away from them as possible! Let them go!

I value who I am, and no one will take me from me.

May 15

As a slave, I worked on the farm with other small boys thinning corn, watching watermelon patches, and later I worked in wheat and tobacco fields. The slaves never had nor earned any cash money.

—James V. Deane a former slave

It is estimated that between eight and 50 million Africans were *sold* into slavery. The average age of Africans shipped abroad was 14. In 1500, Ponce de Leon *purchased* men, women and children in Africa and shipped them to Puerto Rico to harvest sugar cane. Men, women and children bought in Africa were also *sold* in Cuba, Brazil and Haiti to Spaniards who had invaded those countries. And even though Africans, Indians and African-Americans who were enslaved were said to be inferior and not human, it wasn't true. Slavery was not about one group of people being superior and another group inferior. Slavery was about *money*. All that stuff about Africans and blacks being animals and stupid and inferior were lies. Lies told while the slave masters treated them like animals and made mad money off their free labor.

I understand the truth about slavery.

May 16

When you fully claim your history, you can soar.
—George C. Wolfe

Neither your Spanish ancestors, your African ancestors nor your European ancestors were perfect. Africans did wonderful things, but they also did things that were harmful. And yes, it was the Spaniards and other Europeans who invaded Africa, the Americas and the Caribbean and began enslaving human beings. Does that mean if you're Latino, you should be ashamed of your Spanish ancestors? Does that mean if you're of European ancestry you should feel guilty about the horrors of slavery in North America, Latin America and the Caribbean? Does that mean if you're African-American you should be ashamed because your ancestors were slaves? No, it doesn't. Learn the truth and fully claim your history, but celebrate and re-create only what's good about your history. And don't be ashamed about any part of your history. Make peace with the past and with your history. Now soar!

I know who I am, and I'm at peace with the past.

May 17

Somewhere along the line, during the history of this country, many African-Americans decided not to give up during difficult times. If they had, there would be no black families.
—Tyrone P. Dumas

While Africans were enslaved in places like Brazil, Haiti, Puerto Rico, Georgia, North Carolina, Virginia, New York and Texas, they were considered property. In America, slaves picked tobacco, cotton and many crops that made slave owners wealthy. When the slaves worked the fields, metal bits that pressed down on their tongues were placed in their mouths to keep them from talking to each other. Female slaves were raped by their masters. Slaves were named by their owners, but their names were often changed when they were sold so it would be harder for their family members to find them. Horrible, yes, but the story doesn't end there. Many slaves fought back even though they were punished severely. Many ran away. Slavery was devastating for Africans and African-Americans, *but it did not destroy them!* African-Americans are survivors! You are a survivor!

I will persevere during difficult times.

May 18

Look at me! Look at my arm! I have plowed, and planted and gathered into barns and no man could head me!

—Sojourner Truth

Sojourner Truth was born into slavery in New York in 1797. She belonged to several owners before being sold at age 13 to her longtime master, John Dumont. Seventeen years later, her youngest son, Peter, was sold and taken illegally from New York to Alabama. Sojourner sued and got Peter back. That same year in 1827, she ran away from her master and into freedom. In 1843, she changed her named from Isabella Van Wagenen to Sojourner Truth because she said God had called her to travel or "sojourn" and spread the "truth' about slavery and oppression of all kinds. In 1851, Sojourner went to a women's conference to sell copies of her book. The white ministers at the conference, and men throughout the country, said women were inferior. Sojourner told them that she had worked alongside men, been whipped just like the men and was equal to any man! The satellite that orbited Mars in 1997 was named after her.

I am as good as anybody!

May 19

I think that I did well because as a young man, I didn't see any limitations.
—Sidney Gutierrez

You *can* grow up to be president of your country. Benito Juarez became Mexico's president in 1861, the same year Americans began their Civil War and 40 years after Mexico had won independence from Spain. Juarez, an Indian, was born in Oaxaca, Mexico, in 1806. His parents died when he was 3. Juarez lived with an uncle until he was 12. He then went to live with his sister. In 1831, Juarez earned his law degree. He became a judge in 1841, served in his state and national legislatures, and later became Governor of Oaxaca. Juarez's goal was to make Mexico's government fairer for the rich and poor alike, and because of this, he was forced into exile. But he didn't give up. Juarez returned to Mexico and became president! Learn a lesson from Juarez and people like him. Anything is possible, but only if you see possibilities, not limitations.

I can achieve anything I put my mind to.

May 20

The greatest satisfaction is making a difference even if it costs you your life.
—Raul Julia

Eugenio Maria de Hostos, a Puerto Rican journalist, philosopher, lawyer and teacher made a difference. He was born in 1839 in Mayaguez, Puerto Rico. In 1874, Hostos moved to New York and began publishing a newspaper. Later, he moved to the Dominican Republic and published *Las Tres Antillas,* a paper advocating freedom for Puerto Rico, Cuba and the Dominican Republic. When Cuba went to war with Spain in 1895, Hostos fought with the Cubans. He founded a school in the Dominican Republic and he headed two schools in Chile. When the United States took Puerto Rico away from Spain in 1898 after defeating them in the Spanish-American War, Hostos urged Puerto Ricans to decide whether to fight for independence or remain part of the U.S. Hostos died in 1903, one year after Cuba gained its freedom from Spain. Hostos Community College in the Bronx, New York is named after him.

My life matters! I can make a difference!

May 21

The face of America is changing.
—Denise Chavez

Actually, the face of a large part of America used to be the face of Mexico. The Mexican territory, which included New Mexico, Colorado, southern Arizona, California and Texas, began to change as more Americans headed west. Between 1824 and 1830, thousands of Anglo families entered east Texas because they could buy land cheaper there than in the U.S. In 1827, the United States offered Mexico $1 million dollars for the Texas territory. Mexico said no. By 1830, 18,000 whites who owned more than 2,000 slaves had settled in Texas. In the mid-1830s, whites and Mexicans too began calling for secession from Mexico. In 1836, the people in Texas gained their freedom, and Texas became the Lone Star state. In 1845, Texas became the 28th state admitted to the Union and was admitted as a slave state—something many Anglos who moved there wanted all along since slavery was illegal in Mexico.

I am learning all I can about my history.

May 22

Racism either makes you withdraw from yourself, hate yourself or discover yourself.
　　　　　　—Roberto Santiago

After acquiring Texas in 1845, the United States offered Mexico $25 million for the rest of its western territory. Mexico said no. In March 1846, General Zachary Taylor marched soldiers to the border. One month later, the U.S.-Mexican War, known in Mexico as the North American Invasion, was under way. Eighteen months later Mexico had lost the war and its territory from Texas to California. The U.S. and Mexico signed a treaty saying that Mexicans who owned farmland could keep it. But the United States broke the treaty. In 1862, Congress passed The Homestead Act allowing squatters to settle and claim "vacant" lands—lands owned by Mexicans and Indians. Southwestern states passed laws denying Mexicans the right to vote or go to public schools. By the 1900s, lynchings of Mexicans in Texas and California were so rampant that the Mexican ambassador began protesting the racist killings.

The more I learn about racism, the more I discover how wonderful I am.

May 23

What will we have when we have nothing but dependency on those who destroyed us?
　　　　　　　—Pedro Albizu Campos

Five years after a black Puerto Rican, Ramon Emeterio Betances, led a rebellion against Spain, Spain abolished slavery in Puerto Rico. Most slaves had been brought to Puerto Rico from Yoruba in West Africa. In 1898, Spain went to war with the United States. When America won the war and gained control of Puerto Rico, Americans began buying up farms and displacing Puerto Rico's farmers. By 1930, four American corporations controlled three-fifths of Puerto Rico's sugar production, the island's main industry. So Puerto Ricans migrated to America and found work in New York's cigar industry and in Louisiana's sugar fields. In 1917, American citizenship was imposed upon Puerto Ricans although many refused citizenship. That same year, English was decreed the official language of Puerto Rico. In 1933, the Roosevelt administration reversed the policy and Spanish was again the official language.

I am in control of what happens to me.

May 24

Education is the key.
—Tia and Tamera Mowry

During slavery, it was illegal for blacks to learn to read. But many who were enslaved snuck away late at night and taught themselves to read. In 1831, a white woman named Prudence Crandall opened an academy for free black girls in Canterbury, Conn. Her neighbors harassed her and the students, broke the school's windows, poisoned the school's well, and finally, burned the school down. After slavery ended, blacks still couldn't go to public schools or colleges. In 1904, with "five little girls, a dollar and a half, and faith in God," Mary McLeoud Bethune founded the Daytona Educational and Industrial Institute in Florida. The school first taught black students to the eighth grade then it merged with a black school for boys. In 1929, the school became what it is today—Bethune-Cookman College. Bethune-Cookman is one of more than 100 Historically Black Colleges and Universities

I take full advantage of the opportunities I have.

May 25

Don't rush into a decision about college. Give it a lot of consideration.
—Sheryl Swoopes

National Hispanic University (NHU) in San Jose, California and Boricua College in New York are four-year predominantly Hispanic Universities. NHU was founded in 1981 by Dr. Roberto Cruz. Boricua College was founded in 1974 by Dr. Victor G. Alicea, and has campuses in New York City There are great predominantly black and predominantly Hispanic universities out there, just like there are excellent majority-white universities. And you'll ponder many different factors when deciding what school is best for you. One thing you can do is call professionals already doing what you want to be doing, and ask them where they went to school. Don't be afraid to call them up. They'll probably be thrilled to hear from you and thrilled to tell you about their experiences.

I am carefully considering which college is best for me.

May 26

Many people wonder at the crime wave sweeping our country.

—Ida B. Wells-Barnett

The summer of 1919 was called "Red Summer" because from April to October, there were race riots in 25 cities. Twenty-three blacks and 15 whites died and more than 500 people were injured. That same year, 78 blacks were lynched. Ida B. Wells-Barnett, a teacher, journalist and activist spent her life fighting against black lynchings. In 1892, three close friends of Wells' opened People's Grocery Store, in a predominantly black section of Memphis, Tenn. across the street from a white-owned store. The white store owners became upset because they lost business to People's, and fights broke out. One night, during a riot, three deputies were wounded. People's owners and many others were arrested and jailed. Several days later, People's owners were killed. After Wells wrote about the lynchings in the *Memphis Free Speech*, the newspaper's headquarters were destroyed. But Wells continued to speak out against lynchings, and write about lynchings for several newspapers.

I will speak out against wrong.

May 27

We must know where we came from in order to know where we're going.
—Rosa Guerrero

Two months before entering World War I in 1917, the United States passed the Immigration Act specifically to keep northern and southern Europeans from coming to America. But the act kept people from all countries from immigrating. Because so many men served in the war, there weren't enough Americans to work on farms, so Congress let Mexican workers immigrate despite the act. When the stock market crashed in October 1929 and subsequently, the Great Depression began, Americans forced Mexicans back to Mexico because they didn't want to compete with them for the few jobs available. History repeated itself during World War II when, once again, America's entrance into the war caused a labor shortage, and Mexicans were called back to the United States. Mexicans worked in steel factories, meat-packing plants, utility companies and on farms.

Understanding my country's past helps me understand the present and prepare for the future.

May 28

If you believe in something strongly enough, you can make it happen. That doesn't mean you can't improve on it or take advice from people, but don't give up on your dream.

—Bob Williams

In 1942, the first of 992 college graduates began training at Tuskegee Institute in Alabama to become World War II fighter pilots. Bob Williams was part of the first class of trainees who came to be called The Tuskegee Airmen. The Tuskegee Airmen flew alongside planes carrying bombs and fought off enemy planes trying to shoot down the bombers. They flew 1,578 missions, won 150 Distinguished Flying Crosses, 744 air medals and *never* lost a bomber to enemy fire. The people in control thought the Tuskegee Airmen would fail because they believed blacks were inferior and too dumb to fly planes. In 1952, Bob Williams wrote a screenplay about the Tuskegee Airmen and tried to sell it. Some 40 years later, after hearing no, no, no, Williams finally heard a yes and sold his film. He had the kind of determination it takes to succeed and to produce great works like *The Tuskegee Airmen*.

I know I've got what it takes to make my dreams come true.

May 29

Finally, many Negroes have come to believe that they are being exploited politically and economically by the white "power structure."
>—From the Kerner Commission
> Report of 1968

From 1932 to 1972, black men in Macon County, Ala. were purposefully denied medical treatment for syphilis so U.S. government doctors could learn more about how the disease affected human beings. The experiment, called The Tuskegee Study, was conducted by the Public Health Service and it involved approximately 430 mostly illiterate and uneducated black men aged 25 and up. The men were examined by doctors and told they had "bad blood," and they were led to believe they were being treated for whatever they had. The men thought bad blood meant that they were sick with something, but not specifically syphilis. Many of the men died from syphilis. Others went blind or insane. Tuskegee Institute approved of the experiment from the beginning and allowed its hospital and some of its staff to help with the study. The study ended in 1972 only after it was reported about in the newspaper.

I am educated and will not be exploited!

May 30

We've got to let our young kids know that they're where they are today because somebody suffered.
　　　　　　　　　　　—Hank Aaron

Boycotts and protests by African-Americans didn't begin in 1955 with Rosa Parks. In the late 1930s, Adam Clayton Powell, Jr., helped organize Harlem blacks who boycotted the telephone company, a bus company and retail stores on 125th Street until each of them began hiring blacks. In 1917, two years before Red Summer, Harlemites took to the streets and marched in a silent parade to protest lynchings. A year earlier, Jamaican-born Marcus Garvey had introduced his Universal Negro Improvement Association (UNIA) in Harlem. Garvey's group called for black pride, financial independence and self-rule for blacks. He wanted blacks to go back to Africa because he believed African-Americans could never find justice in America. In 1922, he asked the League of Nations to give the UNIA control of the African countries then under Germany's control. But three years after his request, Garvey was convicted of mail fraud, and in, 1927 he was deported.

I'm thankful for all of those who paved the way for me.

May 31

I love the phenomenon of being an American because it's not just my history—my history is right up there next to everybody else's. People that are very different than me, even if we have violent connections—we each complete each other's story.
—George C. Wolfe

In Los Angeles in the 1940s, Mexican-American teenagers began wearing drapes, which resembled zoot suits worn in Harlem. Whites began calling the teenagers "Zoot Suiters" in newspaper and magazine articles, and they blamed them for the city's rising crime rate. On June 3, 1943, 11 sailors on leave got into a fight with men they thought to be Mexican. The next day, 200 sailors in taxis drove through Mexican-American neighborhoods and beat up men who looked Mexican. *The police didn't get involved.* By June 7, many civilians had joined the riot, and African-Americans and Filipinos were also being attacked. Finally, the sailors were forbidden to go downtown. A citizen's committee found that racism caused the riots, and newspaper articles and police inaction encouraged and allowed the riots to continue.

Each day, I discover more and more about my country's history.

June 1

In Chattanooga, Tennessee, as a kid, I saw signs that said No Niggers and Dogs.
—Samuel L. Jackson

Before becoming an actor and starring in movies *like Pulp Fiction,* and *"Die Hard 3,* Samuel L. Jackson, like many college students in the 60s and 70s, became involved in campus protests. During his sophomore year, Jackson was one of 30 students expelled for locking up Morehouse College's board of trustees after administrators wouldn't meet with them. The students were demanding that the school offer a black studies program. Although expelled, Jackson was later readmitted to Morehouse. Like many black kids, Jackson grew up seeing racist signs. And, in states from Texas to California, Mexican kids saw signs that read, "No Niggers, No Mexicans, No Dogs." But boycotts and marches and yes, protests by Mexicans, Puerto Ricans, African-Americans, whites, Asians and Native Americans caused those signs to come down and the laws that supported those signs to change.

Together, we can change our society and our world.

June 2

I get angry. There's resentment in me. You think life's supposed to be fair, but you're always found to be less equal somehow.
—John Leguizamo

If you're Latino or African-American, there are probably times when you feel you aren't being treated equally. Like when you get followed around in stores by salespeople. Or when you think you're being punished by your teacher for the same thing another kid did but didn't get punished for. And, just like John, you're probably resentful. As you've learned by reading the preceding pages, blacks and Hispanics have had it rough in America. And even though things have changed since the time of the Zoot Suit riots of the 1940s and the lynchings of Red Summer, racism is still a reality. You can get angry about racism but you can't stay angry. Turn your anger into activism, and don't let racism defeat you. Don't ever let someone's actions or attitudes make you think you're no good. You are *not* less equal! Still, you won't always be treated fairly. But you cannot let racism and discrimination defeat you.

Racism is a reality, but it will not defeat me.

June 3

I went through my own angry period. I don't want to be angry. okay, fine—racism exists. We were enslaved. Let's go on. I'm living right here, right now.

—N'bushe Wright

It's time to move on. It's time to decide that the past is over and the future is yet to be! And since the future hasn't come yet, why not make the most of the present? If you concentrate on making the present good, you can create a wonderful future for yourself. How do you do this? Get control of your mind. Get control of your thoughts. Get control of your actions. Yes, learn all you can about your past, your history, but don't get stuck in it. Forgive! Let go. Stop being so upset over the past. Turn your anger about the past into positive activism in the present. People who go through life *angry* about racism are miserable, defeated people who feel hopeless about their past present and future. And that's no way to live your life. Like N'bushe said, it's time to do what you've got to do *right here, right now*.

I am living in the present!

June 4

A lot of my friends were sniffing glue, then they were smoking pot, a month later they were heroin addicts, and six months later they were dead.
　　　　　—Jellybean Benitez

Anybody who thinks that smoking weed can't lead you into other drugs like crack and heroin—think again. Fortunately for Jellybean Benitez, and for us, he didn't choose drugs. He followed his dreams and his passions and became the president of a bilingual Spanish/English music label. Benitez, a Puerto Rican, grew up in the South Bronx, dropped out of high school, then began deejaying at New York City clubs. His talent led him to producing CDs for Madonna and Whitney Houston. Next, Hollywood began utilizing his talents by paying him to supply just the right music for films such as *The Perez Family* and *Mi Vida Loca*. Guess what? You have talent too! There's a special gift you've been given by your creator, and it's up to you to figure out what it is. You'll never discover your talent, however, if you're always faded. You'll never develop your talent if you spend your time with drugs and 40s.

I use the talents my creator gave me.

June 5

When my parents came to this country, they had the feeling that the next generation would be better.
—Mary Rodas

Mary's parents were right! She is doing better than they did. At age 13, Mary Rodas began working for a toy company, Catco, Inc. How? Mary's parents came to the United States in 1971 knowing very little English. Her mother cleaned houses part time and her father got a job as a building superintendent. When Mary was 4 years old, she went with her father to work as he checked on a luxury high-rise building in Union City, N.J. They stopped by the apartment of a businessman who was putting new tiles on his kitchen floor. Mary told the businessman that he wasn't matching the tiles correctly. Surprised by her honesty and her eye for detail, he made her a *paid toy consultant.* He gave her toys to play with, and she told him whether or not kids would like them. A few years later, Mary helped design the hugely successful Balzac Balloon Ball. By the time she was 18, Mary was making $200,000 as a V.P. at Catco, Inc.

My life keeps getting better and better!

June 6

I don't want anyone out there to give up. I'm a prime example of being down and getting back up.
—Heather B.

Heather B. was one of six cast members on MTV's first installment of *The Real World*. When her first single, "I Get Wreck" wasn't a smash hit, she fell on hard times financially. But she didn't give up. She went from having her electricity and her phone turned off to opening a hair salon, Nubian Nails and Hair. The New Jersey native then went about resurrecting her singing career and signed a contract with a record company and a major distributor. When you set goals for yourself, you have to be determined to see them through to the end. And you have to understand that it takes time to reach your goals. You'll never reach your goals, though, if you give up the first time you run into problems or the first time you hear the word *no* or the first time it seems as though you've failed. If you want to accomplish something, you have to stick with it even when it may seem like you're not going to make it.

I'm here to stay.

June 7

You get up. You get in the car. You drive out there and make something happen.
—Everett Hall

Everett Hall has been making things happen since he was a teenager. One Easter, Everett couldn't find any dress pants he liked. So, at age 13, instead of buying pants he didn't like, he spent two weeks making his own pair. Several months later, Everett began making clothes for family, friends and neighbors. At Howard University, Everett made and sold clothes to classmates. Since 1994, Everett and his brother, Edwin, have been selling their Everett Hall designer label clothes for men in a Washington DC boutique. Their client list has included Alonzo Mourning, Charles Barkley, Barry White, Maury Povich and Grant Hill. Since 1992, they've made more than one million dollars each year. And business keeps getting better! If you want something to happen, and happen big, start while you're young and do what Everett did—get up, get out there and make it happen.

I make good things happen!

June 8

But let justice roll down like waters and righteousness like a mighty stream.
—Amos 5:24

Dr. Martin Luther King Jr. used the above Bible verse in his historic March on Washington speech, August 28, 1963. This quote uses an analogy or a comparison to make a point. When used in writing and literature, analogies are called similes and metaphors. Similes are good devices because they allow readers to form mental pictures of what a writer is trying to say. In this case, we picture justice and righteousness as being too powerful to be stopped or denied—which is exactly the point Dr. King was making about justice for blacks in America, that it could not be held back. Similes and metaphors are effective writing devices, but they're just two of several tools used by writers to keep you reading to the end of the book. On the following pages, you'll learn about some wonderful writers and about the world beyond what you see on TV and at the movies.

I am open to new ideas and new thoughts.

June 9

What I'm saying in my writing is that we can be Latino and still be American.
—Sandra Cisneros

In *The House on Mango Street* by Sandra Cisneros, a Chicana teenager named Esperanza Cordero invites us into her world in a predominantly Hispanic section of Chicago. As the book begins, Esperanza's parents have recently bought their first house on Mango Street. Esperanza introduces us to her parents, her sister Nenny, their friends Lucy and Rachel, an immigrant woman longing to return to her country and a neighborhood girl who gets beaten by her father. We go with Esperanza to her first after-school job and to her blind Aunt Lupe's house. We meet fickle friends like Cathy who said she'd be Esperanza's friend until next week when she and her family would be moving. They were moving, Cathy said, because the neighborhood was getting bad. Other books by Cisneros are *Woman Hollering Creek* and *My Wicked Ways*.

I am learning about the world by reading interesting books.

June 10

Life is full of changes, my brother.
—Linda Cameron

Often you're scared of changes, but if you don't change, you'll stop growing and you'll become static. When something is static, it's resting. We all need to rest, but even when it seems as though our bodies and minds are resting, inside, things are still working to keep us new and fresh. That's why your stomach lining replaces itself every five days and your skin replaces itself once a month. While you're reading this, millions of cells in your body are dying out and being replaced by new ones. All of this keeps you alive and healthy. The emotional changes you go through also keep you alive and healthy. You may not always feel good when you're going through emotional changes, but you *will* to go through them. Just remember not to be afraid when you're going through changes. Changes are natural, they're necessary and they allow you become a better person.

I am constantly changing for the better.

June 11

The free man is the man with no fears.
                    —Dick Gregory

At the beginning of *Native Son*, by Richard Wright, the protagonist, or the main character, Bigger Thomas, is afraid. Bigger wants a chance to fly planes, he wants out of poverty and the miserable apartment he lives in with his mother and his brothers and sisters, and he wants desperately to get out of doing another robbery with his friends, Gus, G.H. and Jack. His fear of being killed while committing another crime overwhelms him, and he starts a fight with one of his friends, thereby making sure the four of them won't go through with their planned burglary. Bigger's fear and his hatred for himself and for the racist society he lives in stays with him throughout the book. Wright, who also wrote, *Black Boy* and *The Long Dream*, divides Native Son into sections, instead of chapters. Section one, or Book One, as Wright labels it, is actually titled "Fear." Book Two is titled "Flight" and Book Three, "Fate." Check it out!

I overcome my fears with faith.

June 12

We don't just take in energy; we are energy.
—Dan Millman

Energy keeps you alive. You get energy from the foods you eat. Plants make their own energy or their own food by absorbing energy from the sun then mixing that energy with carbon dioxide to produce glucose. It's called photosynthesis. You, in turn, eat the plants and the animals that eat plants and you use energy that originated from the sun. You also get energy from other people. Someone who is happy and excited sends out positive energy. Someone who is pissed off and angry sends out negative energy. When you're pissed off or angry, you use up your energy quickly and you feel tired. If you stay angry for a long time, you'll get depressed. Sure you'll get angry sometimes. But, as you've already read, you've got to learn how to let go of your anger. You've got to learn to use your energy wisely.

I give good energy.

And if they murder, it's usually the ones who look like them, the ones closest to who they are—the mirror reflection. They murder and they're killing themselves over and over.

—Luis J. Rodriguez

Luis J. Rodriguez began writing his autobiography, *Always Running/La Vida Loca: Gang Days in L.A.,* in 1969 at age 15. He decided to finish the book in 1992 because his 15-year-old son had entered gang life, and he wanted to do something to help him get out. In his book, Rodriguez writes of growing up amid poverty and racism in the San Gabriel Valley, just outside Los Angeles. By the time he was 18 years old, 25 of Rodriguez's friends had been killed by rival gangs, the police, drugs or car crashes or by committing suicide. Rodriguez writes about the police brutality and racism suffered by Latinos in his community. He also tells how gangs and drugs nearly killed him and his community. Rodriguez escaped the barrio and the gang and became a journalist and later a published author. Luis J. Rodriguez is living proof that there is a way out of poverty, drugs and gang life—the crazy life that leads nowhere!

I can become whomever I want to become.

June 14

Everybody in the band was going through this kind of rebirth and it went from the burdens of being alive to appreciating being alive.
—Eddie Vedder of Pearl Jam

The force that created you doesn't want living to be a burden. That's why you were given everything you need to live a healthy, happy and prosperous life. Your creator gave you a body programmed with cells smart enough to know how to protect you when things go wrong. That's why when you're sick with a cold or a viral infection, your body gets weak. Your body is using your energy to fight off your cold or infection so you have no choice but to chill! You perspire when you exercise because your body has overheated and perspiration, or the water lost through your skin, helps cool you down. Nothing about how your body works is an accident. You are as smart as they come, and you were created for a reason. And even though we've all been given different bodies and different minds to work with, we all have what we need to live our version of a successful, happy life.

I am programmed to live a happy, healthy, successful life.

June 15

Everybody's trying to fit into the mainstream. You know kids can be clique-y. In the past, I've been sort of persecuted and talked about and all that.
—Claire Danes

In *Coffee Will Make You Black* by April Sinclair, teenagers on Chicago's Southside give us a glimpse of what life was like growing up in the turbulent '60s. Though many things have changed since then, many haven't. The main character, Stevie, has to decide whether she'll give it up to her boyfriend. Stevie and her girlfriend, Carla, navigate the oftentimes tricky waters of peer pressure, parents, boys, sex and the need to "fit into the mainstream," like pilot and co-pilot, with Carla leading the way. A year before they became friends, Carla and Stevie got into a fight because Denise, who had pretended to be Stevie's friend, lied and told Carla Stevie had been doggin' her out. You'll laugh and trip with Stevie, Carla, their parents and their classmates as you read *Coffee Will Make You Black*, and you'll see that each generation of teenagers goes through many of the same things.

My friends are loving and supportive.

June 16

I've learned you have to be patient in family matters. Persistent but very patient.
—Victoria Rowell

In *Go Tell It On the Mountain,* James Baldwin tells the story of a family having a hard time showing love for one another. The story, a semiautobiographical tale of Baldwin's life, growing up a preacher's kid, is told through the voice of 14-year-old John Grimes. John hates his father because he's mean to John and favors Roy, John's bother. Roy despises his father, because he's strict and he beats Roy every time Roy gets into trouble, which is pretty often. Both boys are skeptical of their father's religion and his devotion to his religion. Their father, Gabriel, is having a hard time loving his wife and his children because he's holding on to things that happened in the past— things his wife and kids know nothing about. Gabriel's wife, Elizabeth, is also trying to deal with her past and gain forgiveness from God so she can be at peace.

I am patient with my family members because I understand we each have problems to work through.

June 17

My mother was always trying to instill in us the dignity and the pride of people who live without.
—Juanita Chavez, daughter of
Dolores Huerta

In *And The Earth Did Not Devour Him* (Y no se lo trago la tierra), Tomas Rivera writes about the hardships and tragedies suffered by Mexican-American migrant farm workers during the '40s and '50s. Rivera tells his story through the voice of a teenage boy remembering events that happened as he grew up watching his parents and cousins work like slaves in the Texas fields. We learn that many farm workers got sick while picking fruit under the hot sun because they weren't allowed to take enough water breaks. We also learn what happens when a small child, who worked alongside his parents in the fields, snuck to the water tank because he couldn't wait until break time to get a drink. Although their lives were hard, the farm workers always looked for work, they always had their dignity, and they tried to improve their lives even though some died in the process.

I will always have my dignity and I will always be proud of who I am.

June 18

Education is your passport to the future, for tomorrow belongs to the people who prepare for it today.

—El-Hajj Malik El-Shabazz

When Malcolm X, who later became El-Hajj Malik El-Shabazz, was in the eighth grade, his English teacher asked him what he wanted to be when he grew up. Malcolm replied "a lawyer." Malcolm's teacher told him that wasn't a realistic goal for a "nigger." Malcolm didn't become a lawyer. He quit school and became a thug. Shortly before he turned 21, Malcolm was sentenced to ten years in prison for a string of burglaries he'd committed with friends. In prison, Malcolm began reading. The books he read helped shape his opinions and beliefs about race relations. Malcolm began to share his beliefs on the streets of Harlem, and quickly became a leader. He later changed some of his beliefs after he began traveling throughout the world and exposing himself to new ideas. Malcolm told the story of his life in his autobiography, a book about a boy becoming a man—a powerful, intelligent, educated man.

Knowledge is power. I am knowledgeable therefore I am powerful.

June 19

I'm dark, but I'm Puerto Rican.
                    —Lauren Velez

In his poem, "Nigger-Reecan Blues," Willie Perdomo asks the question   Puerto Ricans often get asked, "What are you, Boricua o Moreno, Puerto Rican or black?" Why? Because some Puerto Ricans and some blacks have very similar facial features. In "Nigger-Reecan Blues," Perdomo offers his own special answer to that sometimes bothersome question. Willie Perdomo lives in Harlem and was the 1990 winner of the Nuyorican Poets Cafe Grand Slam. His poems are featured in *In The Tradition: An Anthology of Young Black Writers*, and also in an anthology titled *New New York*. His work also appeared in PBS's Alive From Off Center series titled *Words in Your Face.* You can also check out Willie's own book of poetry titled, *Where a Nickel Cost a Dime.*

I know who I am.

June 20

The initial question of my life was explaining to myself first my mother's absence, and then my father's.

—Edwidge Danticat

Danticat's parents left her when she was a little girl. They fled the violence in Haiti and immigrated to Brooklyn, New York. Danticat joined them when she was 12. In *Krik? Krak!* Danticat writes about the horrors of living in Haiti, the poorest country in the Western hemisphere. In the opening story, "Children of the Sea," a teenage girl and her boyfriend write love letters to each other. She's in Haiti with her family planning how they'll escape. He is on a raggedy boat with 36 other people fleeing Haiti. He escaped when he learned the soldiers were coming to kill him because he got on the radio and spoke out against government corruption. Another 15-year-old girl on the boat got pregnant when she was raped by the soldiers. When her baby was born dead, the others asked her, for several days, to throw it overboard. When she finally agreed, she also jumped overboard and became yet another child of the sea.

Although bad things have happened, writing about them allows me to heal from them.

June 21

After all, Latinos have something unique to offer.
—Jennifer Lopez

Esmeralda Santiago offers her unique voice in the autobiography of her childhood, *When I Was Puerto Rican.* Esmeralda, the oldest of 11 children lived in Macun and Santurce, Puerto Rico, before moving to Brooklyn, NY. When she entered eighth grade in Brooklyn, she couldn't speak English well and was put into a class for learning disabled students—even though she'd made all *A's* in Puerto Rican schools. By the ninth grade, even though she still couldn't speak English well, Esmeralda was reading and writing English at a tenth-grade level! This time, she was put in a class with other smart ninth graders, and later that year she was accepted into New York's Performing Arts High School. Esmeralda went on to earn her undergraduate degree from Harvard and her graduate degree from Sarah Lawrence College.

I am Boricua, and I can do anything anyone else can!

June 22

More people should open their minds up to other options, and I guess the way to do those things is to start reading books and start doing things, and participate in activities that enrich your current situation and enlighten you to what the rest of the world is like.

—Kid Sensation.

For those of you who understand the value of reading and the value of becoming enlightened, here are more books and authors worth checking out:

A Tree Grows in Brooklyn by Betty Smith
Let The Circle Be Unbroken by Mildred Taylor
Kaffir Boy, by Mark Mathabane
Walk Two Moons by Sharon Creech
Yo Soy Joaquin by Rodolfo "Corky" Gonzales
If Beale Street Could Talk by James Baldwin
Catcher in the Rye by J.D. Salinger
I Hadn't Meant To Tell You This by Jacqueline Woodson
I Know Why the Caged Bird Sings by Maya Angelou
M.C. Higgins, The Great by Virginia Hamilton

Each day, I become more and more enlightened.

June 23

I think so many of our young people feel that poetry is something they're going to be tested on and not going to know the right answer.
—Rita Dove

Harlem Renaissance poets, Langston Hughes, Countee Cullen and Claude McKay, wrote about what life was like for blacks during the earlier part of the twentieth century. Evangelina Vigil-Pinon's poetry speaks of family, feminism, childhood and the urban experience. Sonia Sanchez, Nikki Giovanni, Amiri Baraka and June Jordan, poets and activists, came of age during the 1960s. Maya Angelou's *"And Still I Rise"* is a collection of poems, poems which pay tribute to phenomenal women and poems about courage, hope and resilience. Younger poets including Benny Medina, Nicole Breedlove, Kevin Powell, Martin Espada and Kimberly Collins will sometimes kick their poetry in clubs like the one shown in the movie *Love Jones*. Don't fear poetry. There's a lot to be learned from the lines, stanzas and funky, low-down rhythms of the lyrical wordsmiths.

I am open to all knowledge.

June 24

If I had but two loaves of bread, I would sell one and buy hyacinths, for they would feed my soul.
—Ancient Saying

Hyacinths, spring flowers that produce fragrant blossoms shaped like long, curved eyelashes huddled together on a slender stalk, can be blue, pink, white, yellow or purple. Have you ever wondered why flowers are so beautiful? It's because of all their magnificent colors, sure, but why are they created with such wonderful colors? Flowers growing in the wild are colorful because their colors attract the insects that pollinate them. Through pollination, flowers reproduce and create more beauty. You see, there is a reason why *all* things in nature are the way they are. Every living thing has a purpose. When you understand your purpose in life, you can go out and do what it is you're meant to do. When you understand that everything in nature exists for a reason, you'll better appreciate nature, and you'll be less likely to abuse it.

I appreciate the beauty of all living things.

June 25

Injustice stalks the land like a tiger.
—Ken Saro-Wiwa

What's all the fuss about saving the rain forests? Well, because of the mild climate in the rain forests, more than half the animal species known to man live in rain forests. Destroying the rain forests means destroying those animals! Some of the foods we eat come from tropical rain forests—foods like bananas, vanilla and cinnamon. Rubber, an essential ingredient in the sneakers you wear, is also grown in rubber trees found only in rain forests. Additionally, 25 percent of all medicines are made from plants found in the rain forests. Those plants, like the plants growing in your backyard, also produce the oxygen we need to breathe and stay alive. Green plants take in the harmful carbon dioxide we breathe out and they emit the good oxygen we breathe in. So we need the plants to survive and they need us! Word! We need the rain forests a lot more than we need the money made from destroying them.

I protect and respect trees, plants and animals.

June 26

Some might say that the environment is not a black issue, but I worked in Los Angeles and I saw more black and Hispanic children with uncontrolled asthma as a result of pollution.
—Dr. Mae C. Jemison

Our rivers and oceans are just as important as the rain forests. Unfortunately, they're under attack too! Humans first settled along riverbanks after they stopped wandering from place to place to find food. Why? Because when rivers overflow they leave behind areas of rich soil excellent for planting crops and growing food. Factories and mills were built near rivers, because before there was electricity, the force of the water was used to turn windmills that operated machines inside factories. When machines became electrically powered, factories continued to locate along riverbanks, and some factory owners began dumping their waste into rivers. Waste pollutes rivers and destroys the animals. When we dump toxic chemicals into our rivers, we dump toxic chemicals into the fish we eat. When we dump so much waste that we kill all the fish, we'll have no fish to eat!

I am doing my part to keep our rivers and lakes clean.

June 27

People from the projects are stigmatized. Most folks think we don't care about anything. But I want people to understand we do care about our world.
—Hazel Johnson

Whether you live in the projects or in a mansion you need to be concerned about your environment. Why? Because we all breathe the same air so if the air is messed up, no one breathes good air. If the water is polluted, no one can drink it. If you live in a poor neighborhood or a black neighborhood, poor or not, you have to watch your back even more because business people who don't care about you, will try to use your neighborhood as their personal dumping ground. It's called environmetal racism. And people who live near factories that pollute the air and the water suffer more from diseases like asthma than people who don't. Word! Be an environmental activist! How? Don't throw trash on the streets. Recycle your soda cans and bottles. And never let anyone come into your neighborhood and mess it up.

I care about my neighborhood and about the air I breathe.

As long as the moon shall rise, As long as the rivers shall flow, As long as the sun shall shine, As long as the grass shall grow.

> —Common expression in treaties
> Between Native Americans
> and white men

Native Americans worship the earth. They also worship and respect the sun, the moon, the wind and the rain. When Africans were brought to America and enslaved, some married into Native American communities. Anthropologists estimate that as many as 25 percent of all blacks in America have some Native American ancestry. When Native Americans retaliated against whites who had abused them and taken their land, Africans and blacks were usually not harmed in the attacks. And Native Americans frequently housed runaway slaves, some of whom stayed to raise families within the Indian tribe. Still, some blacks also settled on land stolen from Native Americans. And some black soldiers helped capture Native American chiefs and tribal leaders along with white men. Also, some Native American tribes like the Cherokee had African slaves.

I am learning more and more about my ancestry.

June 29

Ten years from now I want to be living on a ranch in
Mexico or the Arizona desert, coaching Little League
baseball and raising my kids.
—Frost

Where do you want to be 10 years from now? If you
haven't thought about where your life is headed, why
not? There's an old saying, "You gotta have a dream
if you're gonna make your dream come true!" If you
don't have dreams and goals, get some! Don't be
afraid to dream! And don't be afraid to really believe
in your dreams! There's another saying, "Be careful
what you wish for because you may get it!" Most of
what you hope and wish for does come true. The
problem is too many people are wishing for the
wrong things! You're afraid of bad things happening
and oftentimes, you think about the worst possible
things that could happen. Sometimes your fears turn
out to be nothing, but other times, you bring about
the very things you're afraid of because you think
about them so much. Dream good dreams! Then do
whatever you must to make your dreams come true.

I am courageous enough to dream!

June 30

I wasn't even thinking of hurting anyone when the night began. But we both fought to protect our reputations. We felt we had to do that to keep other people from disrespecting us.
—Darius Davis

Many kids get into fights! So do many adults! Nowadays, fights between kids often turn deadly. Why? Because nowadays, some kids carry guns. Some who carry guns are scared. They're scared of the other kids out there who have guns, and they want to feel safe and protected. It's no fun walking around scared all the time. It's also no fun to be disrespected in front of your friends. But if you choose to carry a gun and if you choose to use a gun to settle a fight or an argument or to get revenge, you've got to be prepared for the consequences. Every day, you hear about the consequences of gun use by teenagers. Unfortunately, violence by youth is increasing, and too many of you say you don't feel safe. But things have got to change, because if they don't, soon, everybody will have a gun, and instead of everyone feeling safe and protected, no one will!

I am a peaceful person.

July 1

I don't think our young people really are looking forward to dying from AIDS or guns by age 21. They'll take better alternatives if we make them available.
—Marian Wright Edelman

They are trying! No, the world you're living in is not perfect and yes, adults have made a mess of things. But there are adults who are trying to fix the mess! Adults who recognize we've got to help make your world safer. Adults like Marian Wright Edelman who started the Children's Defense Fund in 1973 to make sure the federal government does right by you! She pushes for jobs for youth, money for pregnancy prevention programs and the passage of laws that protect you. She also organized the 1996 Stand for Children rally in Washington, D.C. Geoffrey Canada, president of the Rheedlan Centers for Children and Families in New York City is also doing his part. One of Geoffrey's many duties is teaching kids how they can avoid violent confrontations. These are just a few of the many adults trying to make things better for you. They are trying!

There are adults out there trying to make the world better for me.

July 2

Get close to good people and you will be one of them. *Arrimate a los buenos y seras uno de ellos.*
—Mexican saying

Are there people you respect and look up to because of the good things they do? Then get close to them! And remember, people who do good things come in all shapes and sizes and colors. Good people and people who do good things aren't perfect people. There are no perfect people. And even good people make mistakes and mess up sometimes. I know you've heard you're supposed to learn from adults' mistakes. The way it usually works though is that you have to make your own mistakes before you really learn your lessons. That's life! But you can make things easier on yourself by hanging with positive people and with people who are doing the right things. Why? Because you tend to act like and be like the people you hang with. Get close to good people and you *will* be one of them!

I hang with people who are doing good things.

July 3

We don't want people cheering. We don't think an audience should get an adrenaline rush when they see violence. So many of those big Hollywood movies glorify violence, sensationalize it.

> —Allen Hughes, director Menace
> II Society and Dead Presidents

If you're tired of all the violence in movies, check out the ones listed below. And if you run across violence in a few of these films, understand that you'll learn about a whole lot more than violence by the time the movie's finished.

o *The War* starring Kevin Costner and Elijah Wood.
o *Stand and Deliver* starring Edward James Olmos
o *Once Upon a Time When We Were Colored*, starring Phylicia Rashad.
o *My Family/Mi Familia* with Jimmy Smits and Esai Morales
o *Hoop Dreams*, a documentary film starring Arthur Agee, William Gates and their families.

I feed my mind with positive images.

July 4

If you had lived during the days of Paul Robeson would you live his life?
—Lyric by Bernice Johnson Reagon

Paul Robeson, born in 1898, was fierce! He stood up to U.S. government officials, and he fought against injustice all over the world—using his principles and his intellect instead of a gun. Robeson went to Rutgers University where he won awards in oratory, lettered in 12 sports, was an All-American football player and graduated with honors. He then began acting in the theater and studying law at Columbia University. After graduating, he joined a New York law firm. He resigned that same year after being told he'd never try cases before a judge because he was black. Not long afterward, Robeson's acting and singing career took off and, in 1926, he toured the United States, sang Negro spirituals and refused to sing in any concert hall where blacks were made to sit in segregated seats.

I stand firm on my principles.

July 5

If you direct your passion toward the highest good of all people, that is the best fuel.
—Carlos Santana

Luisa Capetillo, born in Arecibo, Puerto Rico, in 1879, had a passion for life and for making life the best it could be for everybody. Like Sojourner Truth, Luisa fought for the rights of women as well as men. Luisa was a writer and union leader who believed people should be paid good wages and that good wages would mean happier families, better educational opportunities for kids and less violence in the home. In 1907, she joined a tobacco factory strike in Puerto Rico. A year later, she became an active member in the Federation of Free Workers and two years later, a reporter for the organization's newspaper. She wrote essays about worker's rights that she compiled into a book. In 1910, she founded a newspaper titled, La Mujer (The Woman). Luisa died of tuberculosis in Rio Piedras, Puerto Rico, at age 42.

I have a passion for doing right by people.

July 6

I'll get a chair, drag it up, and sit at the table and make sure my voice is heard.
　　　　　　—Wilma Mankiller

Before his death in 1993, Cesar Chavez's voice was heard many times as he spoke up for migrant farm workers. Born in 1927 near Yuma, Ariz., Chavez lived with his parents on a 160-acre farm until he was 10. His family moved to California and became migrant farm workers after losing their farm during the depression. After serving in World War II, Chavez settled in Delano, Calif., and, in 1958 formed the National Farm Workers Association. In 1968, the renamed United Farm Workers of America urged Americans to boycott grapes. Before the boycott, the mainly Mexican laborers harvesting the grapes were making 10 cents an hour, working 10-hour days, and they had no union to ensure they'd be treated fairly. Two years after the boycott began, farm owners agreed to a union contract. Unfortunately, migrant farm workers are still being exploited despite the battles won by Chavez and others decades ago.

I have something important to say!

July 7

Ninety-nine percent of the time, in this society, black women never get their due.
—Thelma Golden

Listed below are some black and brown women you may not have heard of. If you don't know who they are, go to the library, look them up, and give them their due!

Luisa Moreno
Lydia Cabrera
Sara Estela Ramirez
Antonia Pantoja
Anna Julia Cooper
Elizabeth Ross Haynes
Dorothy Boulding Ferebee
Hallie Brown
Daisy Lampkin
Biddy Mason
Gloria T. Hull
Sarah Mapps Douglass
Annie Turnbo Malone

You Go Girls!!!

July 8

We're sick and tired of being sick and tired.
—Fannie Lou Hamer

Fannie Lou Hamer, born in 1917 to sharecroppers, began sharecropping at age six. In 1962, Hamer met Southern Christian Leadership Conference (SCLC) workers and Student Non-violent Coordinating Committee (SNCC) workers and said good-bye to sharecropping. She joined the voter-registration movement, and along with 17 others, tried to register. They were required to copy and explain part of Mississippi's Constitution in order to register. (This tactic, used to keep blacks from their legal right to vote, was outlawed in 1964.) Each of them failed! But Hamer didn't give up. She passed the test on her third try. Hamer was arrested and jailed while trying to integrate a Whites Only restaurant. She was then beaten by two black male prisoners who were told if they didn't beat her, they'd get an even worse beating. Hamer continued to protest and organize, and she didn't stop until she died of cancer at age 60.

I give my time and energy to fight for things that are right and against things that are wrong.

July 9

We dare defend our rights.
                              —Alabama state motto

The Civil Rights Memorial in Montgomery, Ala. was dedicated in November 1989. The memorial is located in front of the Southern Poverty Law Center, an organization that tracks hate groups. It lists the names of men—black and white—as well as young girls and teenage boys who were killed during the civil rights struggle. Emmett Till, a teenager, murdered by whites in Money, Miss, because they said he flirted with a white girl in a local store is listed. The memorial also lists landmark events of the civil rights struggle, where men and women, black, white, brown, red, yellow, straight and gay marched and fought and died for freedom and equal treatment under the law. Maya Lin, the architect who designed the memorial, also designed the Vietnam Veterans Memorial. Lin was a 21-year-old Yale University student when she submitted the winning entry in a contest to design the Vietnam memorial.

I remember those who died so that I could be free.

People don't even know about SNCC. Jim Crow would not have been overthrown if it wasn't for student groups like SNCC.

—Ras Baraka, poet and activist

In 1956, people involved with the Montgomery bus boycott formed the Southern Christian Leadership Conference (SCLC) and elected 26-year-old Dr. Martin Luther King, Jr., their president. The boycott ended the discrimination blacks faced when riding city buses. In 1960, SCLC executive director, Ella Baker, met with a group of students at Shaw University and the Student Non-violent Coordinating Committee (SNCC) was formed. Two months earlier, students from A & T University in Greensboro, N.C. had staged a sit-in at F.W. Woolworth's lunch counter. Although blacks could shop at Woolworth's, they couldn't eat there. Soon, students at Morehouse, Fisk Florida A & M, and students in Arkansas, Alabama and New York either stepped up their efforts to stage sit-ins or decided they'd begin. Baker helped the students get organized and SNCC and its students became an integral part of the civil rights struggle.

I will do whatever is necessary to protect my rights.

July 11

As black people, we often use music as an escape from our problems. Yet black artists often forget that music can be used as a form of social protest.
—Amel Larrieux of Groove Theory

When blacks gathered in churches to plot their strategy for marches and boycotts, they sang freedom songs to inspire and encourage them for the battle ahead. When blacks were arrested by the hundreds for staging marches and sit-ins, they'd sing in jail and drive the police crazy with their singing. They sung old Negro spirituals and added new lyrics relating to the civil rights struggle. When SNCC came to Albany, Ga., Bernice Johnson joined the struggle and was arrested, jailed and suspended from Albany State College. In 1962, Bernice, along with Charles Neblett, Rutha Mae Harris and Cordell Hull Reagon became the Freedom Singers—a group established by SNCC to travel throughout the country to raise money for the movement and inspire the protesters. Bernice Johnson Reagon went on to form the world-renowned a capella singing group, *Sweet Honey in the Rock.*

My song is one of freedom and courage and justice!

July 12

The most important thing I've learned is that kids can make a difference. Knowledge is the key, knowledge is the power. Take that power and bring about change.

—Craig Keilburger

In 1954, nine Supreme Court justices voted unanimously to end school segregation. In 1957, nine black students put the Court's decision to one of several nationally televised tests. Arkansas Governor Orval Faubus refused to obey the Court's decision. When he learned black teenagers would try to integrate Central High School in Little Rock, he called the National Guard to stop them. After being denied for several weeks, the students entered the school on September 23. Violence erupted as angry white people beat up blacks and also reporters, photographers and TV people, most of whom were white. Later that day, the students were secretly taken out of school for fear they'd be killed. The next day, President Eisenhower sent 1,000 paratroopers to Central. On September 25, the students, known as the Little Rock Nine, were escorted to school by armed guards.

We will not be denied!

July 13

I would take nigger all the time. 'Nigger, nigger, nigger, nigger, nigger. Black son of a—you black nigger' and all of that. I'll take that any day before I stay in Chicago and sell drugs.

—Arthur Agee star of Hoop
Dreams

Question: How many options do you have in life when considering what you'll do with your life? Answer: You have as many as you think you do! If you think your only options are to sell drugs, rob convenience stores or have kids, then those will be your only options. If you decide your choices are unlimited and you can step out into the world and be whatever you want, then you'll find yourself out in the world doing what you want! That can be scary because the world can be cruel. Arthur Agee put up with the world's ignorance because he wanted a better life for himself. He went away to college in a small town and got called a nigger—many times. He could have been called a lot worse! You see, he's not a nigger and he knew that. But if he had stayed in Chicago and sold drugs and gotten caught, convicted, and carted off to prison, he'd be called a felon!

I am making smart choices about my future.

July 14

Black man, black man you are strong, caring and wise.

> —Someone who knows the real
> deal

You have been lied to and lied about. There are not more young black men in prison than in college. All black male teens are not drug dealers. You haven't all abandoned your responsibilities as teenage fathers. You, black man, are strong, caring and wise. Your African ancestors were great thinkers, great warriors, and great leaders. Your African-American ancestors were great inventors, teachers, peace makers, scientists, politicians and activists. Each of you has a quick mind that allows you to make it in an oftentimes cruel and destructive world. But don't settle for just making it—anybody can do that. You have the power and the wisdom and the desire to be great—to do great things. And it's time for you to begin affirming your greatness. Greatness is you! Don't let anyone stop you from doing great things.

I am strong, caring and wise.

July 15

Latino brothers, you are honorable, responsible and wise.

> —Someone who looks beyond stereotypes

Even though popular culture would have us believe that most Puerto Ricans, Mexicans, Dominicans and Panamanians are lazy, irresponsible gangstas, you know it's not true. Many of you are honorable, responsible and wise. You're not all a bunch of illegal immigrants causing trouble and stealing jobs from Americans. All of you aren't high school drop outs. You haven't all abandoned your responsibilities as teenage fathers. Don't ever doubt your value to society. Don't ever doubt your specialness. Continue to follow the examples of your parents and grandparents who have a strong sense of family and have worked triple overtime to make it in this country.

I am honorable, responsible and wise.

July 16

Beautiful black sista you make the world a better place.

> —Someone who refuses to believe the hype

Try to imagine a world without black women and girls, but don't try too hard because you'll quickly get depressed. Since the beginning of civilization, black women have showered the world with their beauty, their love and their wisdom. Civilization begins with you, black girl! Years ago, in societies across the vast African continent, women chose the tribe's leaders. And even though that tradition didn't last, African-American women and girls continue to make smart choices, and continue to thrive in an oftentimes hostile and misguided world. There are too many lies floating around about you black girl. Lies that say you aren't beautiful, lies that say you're all welfare queens, lies that say you're dumb. You, black girl, are a spiritual creation with a quick mind and a heart full of love. Don't ever doubt your beauty, your love and your wisdom.

I am beautiful, loving and wise.

July 17

Latinas are beautiful people.
—Someone who knows the truth

There are many well-kept secrets about Latinas. Guess what? It's not true that you're all strung out on crack, making babies and running with the fellas in gangs. While others are going off to college, some of you are postponing college to help raise younger brothers and sisters. You've been caring for your siblings since you became teenagers and your strong sense of family compels you to help out when needed. Don't ever let anyone tell you you're not as good as the next person. You are loving, nurturing, intelligent, strong beautiful people. Your beauty lives inside you and radiates outward for the world to see.

I am beautiful, giving and wise.

July 18

They call me Asian, but do they even know what that means?

> —Someone who can help you
> understand

Some people stereotype Asians by calling them the model minority, meaning the best of all minorities. First of all, Asians aren't even Asians. They're Chinese, Japanese, Koreans, Filipinos, Vietnamese, Polynesians, Hawaiians, Samoans, Cambodians, Guamanians, Tongans, Hmong, Malaysians, Thai, Laotians, Indonesians and Asian Indians. Their ancestors, the people from the east, have given the world so many wonderful things. They've shown us how our minds, bodies and spirits can work together to give us long, balanced, peace-filled lives. They're still trying to show people in the west—especially in America—a better way to heal our bodies and practice medicine. And there's a lot more we can learn from them once we stop stereotyping them and we get to know them as individuals!

I am wonderful, wise and filled with inner peace.

July 19

They have a picture of my body on their baseball uniforms, but can they picture my spirit?
—Someone who knows her spirit

You've been murdered, raped and put on reservations. Your image has been distorted like a cartoon and sewn onto baseball, basketball and football uniforms. You've been robbed of many material things, but you know that as long as you keep your spirit, you'll be just fine. You are Cherokee and Ute and Shawnee and Choctaw and Seminole and Pawnee and—*there are more than 100 Indian tribes in America!* Unlike so many others, you worship the land. You understand that no one person or group owns the land we call Mother Earth, and that we were all meant to share it. That's why you take from mother earth only what you need to survive. You've been an example for all to follow, but not enough of us have. Thank you for protecting our home, and thank you for your beautiful spirit.

I honor my spirit even when others try to harm it.

July 20

I'm a white person, and *I know* no one can take my power from me.

> —Someone who understands what
> *real* power is.

As a group, white people have been blamed for a lot bad things. Many people find it very easy to look at history and point to all the bad things white people have done. No matter what history says, you know you're filled with love and wisdom and power! That's right, you've got the power. You've got the money, the land, and you rule corporations. The money, the land and the being in charge represent one kind of power. But there *is* another kind of power that's even greater! The power you have inside. *The power everyone has inside.* The kind of power that can never be taken away. The kind of power that would never kill for land or enslave for money or pollute for corporate greed. When you use the power you have inside—*the power of love*—you can never do bad things!

I am powerful, loving and wise.

July 21

What is true of minorities is that we are not in power, we're not in control of the legislative process. But that does not mean we are not fighting back.
—Rep. Nydia Velazquez

In 1963, Reies Lopez Tijernia organized a movement called *Alianza Federal de las Mercedes* (Federal Alliance of Land Grants) and demanded the return of millions of acres of land formerly owned by Latinos in New Mexico, Colorado, Utah, Texas and California. Tijernia and his followers had many confrontations with the Army and with state troopers as they tried to reclaim land taken from their ancestors. On July 4, 1966, Tijernia led a 62-mile march from Albuquerque, New Mexico to Santa Fe, New Mexico, and he presented Arizona's governor with a petition. In his petition, Tijernia claimed to represent 6,000 Mexican-Americans who were direct heirs of land that had been illegally taken from their ancestors. Tijernia was eventually jailed and given a two-to-ten year sentence for trying to take over part of the Kit Carson National Forest in New Mexico.

I will always fight for my rights and my freedom.

July 22

Our Cuban poet laureate Jose Marti once wrote a letter to his daughter saying, 'My girl, dress simply and modestly. She who carries a lot inside dresses discreetly on the outside.'
—Albita Rodriguez

Jose Marti was not only Cuba's beloved poet, he was a newspaper publisher, an essayist, a children's magazine publisher and a revolutionary. When Cuba was still ruled by Spain, Marti was convicted of disloyalty to Spain and deported to Spain (his parents' homeland) at age 16. He earned philosophy and law degrees while there and he published his first book. He then spent time in exile in Mexico, Guatemala and New York where he founded the Cuban Revolutionary Party in 1892. Marti joined the war against Spain and fought alongside General Maximo Gomez and General Antonio Maceo, an African-Cuban. One-third of all Cubans were of African descent, and in his essay "My Race," Marti argued that human beings needed to stop thinking of themselves in racial terms. Marti died in 1895, three years before Cuba won its independence from Spain.

I am free to make the most of my precious, valuable life.

July 23

Tengo Puerto Rico En Mi Corazon (I Have Puerto Rico in My Heart)
　　　—Slogan of the Young Lords Party

The Young Lords Organization began in Chicago as a Puerto Rican street gang. When the gang's leader was sent to jail, he met up with Fred Hampton, a Black Panther Party member. The gang leader left jail and transformed his street gang into a political group like the Black Panther Party. Puerto Ricans in New York also formed a group and became affiliated with the Chicago organization. Not satisfied with Chicago's leadership, the New York group separated from Chicago and became the Young Lords Party. The Young Lords Party operated a free breakfast program out of a church. They also taught Puerto Ricans their history, and they tried to get rid of the racial tensions between Puerto Ricans and blacks (nearly 25 percent of the Young Lords were blacks) and the tensions between light- and dark-skinned Puerto Ricans. You can read more about the Young Lords Party in a book titled *Palante.*

I involve myself with groups that are about something positive.

July 24

We have a terrific civilization that a lot of people don't know about.
—Jose Martinez

Several decades ago, Mexican and Mexican-American students who couldn't speak English were placed in classes for retarded students. Even those who could speak English were expected to fail or drop out of school altogether. As was expected, many did drop out. But in March 1968, 10,000 disgusted Chicano junior high- and high-school students in Los Angeles walked out of schools. The walk outs in L.A. spurred students in Colorado, Texas and Arizona to follow suit. The students demanded the same educational opportunities they saw whites and blacks getting. They demanded that their history be taught in Chicano studies classes, and they demanded an end to racism. The walk outs became part of the Chicano Movement and organizations like the Mexican-American Youth Organization, El Movimiento Estudiantil Chicano de Aztlan (MEChA) and La Raza Unida party sprang up.

I belong to a terrific group of people that has overcome many obstacles.

July 25

He had a feeling they were going to kill him.
—Philip Montez

Ruben Salazar, born in Chihuahua, Mexico, grew up in El Paso, Texas, and became a journalist. As a columnist for the *Los Angeles Times*, Salazar wrote about East Los Angeles's Chicano community and was criticized by many people, among them, the sheriff of Los Angeles County who thought Salazar was stirring up Mexican-Americans. On August 29, 1970, more than 20,000 people went to Belvedere Park in East L.A. to protest the Vietnam War. They were mad because more Mexican-Americans were being killed in the war than any other group of soldiers. The demonstration turned into a riot, and Salazar, who was by then also a TV reporter, covered the event. Salazar was sitting in a bar after he'd finished his news coverage when police entered and, without warning, fired tear gas projectiles. Salazar went down. There was an investigation, but authorities said Salazar's death was an accident, and no action was ever taken against the police.

My life matters and it matters how I live my life!

July 26

While mass demonstrations remain the most visible and dramatic means of manifesting our determination to bring about change, it is up to the younger generation to develop new ways of protesting derived out of their experiences.

—Angela Davis

College students, Huey Newton and Bobby Seale formed The Black Panther Party in Oakland, Calif. in 1966. The Panthers believed that the only way for blacks to get rid of racism was through self-defense and self-determination. Dressed in black leather jackets and berets, the Panthers carried pump shotguns at their public rallies. Party members in chapters across America had many shootouts with the police. Several Panthers were killed in the shootouts, and many more were arrested and jailed. Fred Hampton, chairman of the Panthers in Illinois was gunned down in the middle of the night by Chicago police as he slept in his bed. The Panthers believed that their struggle was not against all whites, but against racist whites and racist cops and government officials who discriminated against and murdered blacks.

I am doing my part to bring about change in America.

July 27

Through the adversity of life, we must stay focused and work toward being the very best that we can be.
—Marty Garcia

Teenagers today face more adversity than ever before. You're bombarded with media images that promote violence, drugs, alcohol and sex. Some of you live in homes where drugs, alcohol and violence rule. Even if you don't live in homes filled with violence or substance abuse, you wish your parents, your friends, the world would understand you better. It's no wonder some of you are depressed! You have too many painful feelings bottled up inside. You don't talk about how you're feeling with your parents because you don't think they'd understand. Often, you won't even talk about your feelings with your friends because you're afraid they'll think you're crazy. When you're feeling sad, lonely or depressed, you're also feeling the need to tell somebody! Talk things out with someone you trust or with a licensed therapist. Sure it takes courage. You can do it.

I have the courage to talk about how I'm feeling.

July 28

A sensible son gladdens his father. A rebellious son saddens his mother.

—Proverbs 15:20

Some of you live with your dads. Others of you wished you did. Those of you who live with your mom and spend time with your dad on the weekends oftentimes can't wait to see him. You know he loves you and wants the best for you. And you want him to be part of your life. Even though he and your mom have split up, they both want you to grow up to be responsible. And they're doing everything they know how to teach you responsibility. You won't always agree with the decisions your parents make for themselves and for you. Some of you won't always like your parents even though you never stop loving them. Others of you feel as though you've earned the right to hate your parents. No matter how you feel about your parents, you'd do yourself a great favor if you would realize your parents are doing the best they know how.

I understand that my parents are doing the best they can for me.

July 29

Never get into a potentially dangerous situation without first seriously considering the possible outcomes.
—Alejandro "Alex" Padilla

Let's face it, if you're out with a group of people and you decide to get faded or high, you're putting yourself in a potentially dangerous situation. Too many girls have ended up sexually assaulted, raped or even dead after getting faded with people they thought they could trust. Unfortunately, there are boys and men out there who will abuse girls when they're messed up. *Peer pressure is hard enough to resist when you're sober. It's even harder to resist when you're drunk or high.* Too many boys have gone along with the crowd and done things they might not have done had they not been high. Too many girls have let things happen to them when they were drunk that they wouldn't have allowed if they'd been sober. Just because it's summertime and you want to kick it with your friends doesn't mean you forget about how to be a responsible teen.

I consider the consequences before I get into potentially dangerous situations.

July 30

In kindergarten, my teacher asked me what I wanted to be when I grew up, and I told her a scientist. She said, 'Don't you mean a nurse?' Now there's nothing wrong with being a nurse but that's not what I wanted to be.

—Dr. Mae C. Jemison

Mae Jemison earned a chemical engineering degree and later became a medical doctor. Several years later, Jemison joined NASA's space program and became an astronaut! When August Wilson was 15, he was wrongly accused of plagiarizing a 20-page term paper on Napoleon. The paper was so well written that Wilson's teacher thought Wilson's older sister wrote it. The teacher gave Wilson an *F* even though Wilson showed him the footnotes and bibliography to prove he'd done the work. Wilson tore up the paper, threw it away and walked out of his eighth-grade class—never to return. Instead, he spent his days in the library and *he read everything*! Over the next three decades, Wilson wrote plays—plays including *Fences* and *The Piano Lesson* that won Pulitzer Prizes and made him a rich and famous man!

I know exactly what I can do and I do it!

July 31

The person with talent has no limits.
Quien tiene arte va a todas partes.
—Mexican Saying

You are the person with talent. Yes! You! You were born with it. Now all you need to do is develop it, nurture it and allow it to grow. Can you sing? Then sing! Can you dance? Then dance! Can you act? Then act! Do you like to build things? Design those houses and build great things! Do you like to play the clarinet? Then master it and try your hand at the saxophone! Are you fascinated with science and with how things work? Then nurture your fascination and visit planetariums and science museums. Are you a movie buff? Would you like to one day make and direct movies? Why wait? Write your own script, get that video camera and make that movie now. Everybody, I repeat, *everybody!* was born with creativity! Everybody has their own special talent. Nurture your talent, then watch it grow. You have no limits!

I was born with creativity and talent and I have no limits.

August 1

I felt like an outsider. Not that being multiracial was a problem, but it was confusing. It made me feel separate and different from everyone else. I used to wish I was just one thing or another instead of a mixture of things.
—Mariah Carey

If you're bi or multiracial, you may feel separate and different, just like Mariah did. Your parents have probably talked with you about your identity and about your "race." Society also sends you messages about your "race" and your heritage, as do your friends. Sometimes, you act one way when you're with your friends who share one part of your racial heritage and another way with friends who share a different part of your heritage. But even though your parents, society and your friends may influence how you see yourself, ultimately, that decision is yours. And your ideas and attitudes about who you are may change as you get older. Whatever you decide, don't ever let anyone make you feel inferior because your parents are of different "races" and because you're bi or multiracial.

I am thankful that I am who I am.

August 2

My mother's white family disowned her when she married my father, who is black.
—Adrienne Divens

Adrienne Divens didn't meet her mothers' side of the family until her grandfather died. And as with many biracial kids, Adrienne got called names—names like Oreo and zebra. There is no denying the pain you feel when you are not liked because of your "race." There's no denying the pain of not being accepted by family members or by your classmates because your parents are different races. Sometimes, biracial teenagers make the mistake of thinking they're no good when wack things are said or done to them because they're racially mixed. If your father is black and your mother white, or your father white and your mother Mexican, or your father black and your mother Asian, or whatever your heritage is, you have nothing to be ashamed of! Stop judging people because of their race! Stop judging yourself because of your race.

I am proud of who I am no matter what anyone else thinks!

August 3

We have to understand that dark skin is great. We have to stay strong and love our black skin. We have to get rid of the self-hate problem we've had for years.

—Dennis Haysbert

During slavery, white slave owners fathered many children by their African and African-American slaves. These children were usually a lot lighter in skin color than were children of Africans and blacks. Slave owners considered their so-called "mulatto" or mixed-race children smarter than African and black children. Some slave owners sent their biracial, slave children to Europe to be educated and risked arrest since it was against the law for slaves to be educated. Some slave owners also helped their enslaved kids escape when they got older. And there you have the beginnings of color discrimination among blacks. Lighter-skinned blacks were treated better so blacks wanted their children to be born light skinned. And many believed that light-skinned blacks were superior to dark-skinned blacks. It wasn't true then, and it ain't true now!

I love the color of my skin!

August 4

If our youth associate being smart with being White,
what do they think about being Black?
—Jawanza Kunjufu

There are too many myths, lies and stereotypes
floating around about African-Americans and other
minority groups. If you're smart and black or smart
and Hispanic, you're not "acting white." You're just
smart! White people aren't the only ones who can get
good grades. Your intelligence or your mind is just
like your body and your spirit. All three need to be
fed in order to grow and develop and become
stronger. You feed your body with food and exercise.
You feed your spirit by meditating or praying or by
going to church, the mosque or to synagogue. Well,
you feed your mind by reading and studying, no
matter what color you are! If you think you're not
smart because you're black or Latino, you're wrong.
We've all been given intelligence. And when you use
what you've been given, you don't suddenly turn into
a white person!

It's okay for me to show how smart I am.

August 5

I'm a Cuban-American, but I'm also an African-American. So I'm a product of all those influences.
—Jon Secada

Jon Secada has a healthy attitude about who he is. That's because he knows who he is! The more you understand and accept who you are, the better you'll feel about yourself. Each person alive is a product of all kinds of influences—cultural, religious and then some. For example, if your mother or father is in the military and your family has moved around a lot, you've had different experiences than kids whose parents haven't moved a lot. It's good to have many influences. Some of them will be good, others not so good. As you grow and mature, you'll decide what kind of person you want to be and which influences you'll keep and which influences you'll get rid of. After you've decided who you want to be, you can go about changing those things in your life you can't accept, accepting those things you can't change and being smart enough to know which is which.

I acknowledge everything that's true about my life and my family background.

August 6

The American people think Africa is the jungle, but not all Africans are from the jungle. We're civilized there, too.
—Dikembe Mutombo

There are 52 countries on the continent of Africa, the second largest continent in the world. The western part of the continent has the heaviest population. One-sixth of Africa's people live in Nigeria where there are schools, colleges and tall buildings just like in American cities. North Africa has far fewer people who live in Algeria, Libya, Chad and Egypt. The Nile, the world's longest river, begins in the north and stretches for 4,160 miles through the center of Africa. The Sahara Desert is also in the north. Rain forests are found in Central Africa with one of the world's largest and thickest covering most of the northern part of Zaire. East Africa is mountainous. Mount Kilimanjaro, Africa's tallest mountain, is in Tanzania, in the east. Southern Africa contains the countries of Namibia, Botswana, Mozambique, Zimbabwe and South Africa where, in 1994, Nelson Mandela was elected president after spending 27 years in prison.

There's a lot I don't know, but I'm learning more every day.

August 7

Because a man has injured your goat, do not go out and kill his bull.
—Kenyan Proverb

Payback leads only to more payback. You've heard the saying two wrongs don't make a right. Well there's something called forgiveness that can take the place of payback if you'll let it. People who do you wrong will pay for their wrongs without your help. *Remember, whatever you put out, you get back.* So, when someone does you wrong, you don't have to sit around and plot your revenge. Plotting revenge uses up a lot of energy, and it's wasted energy because you're using it on something negative. The problem with payback is that once you've gotten revenge by doing something bad to someone, you have to be prepared for something bad to come back to you. Word! You could skip the revenge and the harmful side affects. How? Try forgiveness! Forgiveness puts an end to payback.

Each day I am more and more forgiving.

August 8

Truth stands the test of time; lies are soon exposed.
—Proverbs 12:19

Sooner or later, a lie is found out. Men and women who make mad money in the cigarette industry got caught lying. For years, they told us cigarettes didn't cause cancer. They said they never spiked cigarettes with high levels of nicotine to get people hooked. They also said that their ads directed at teens didn't entice teens to smoke. In 1995, they testified before Congress and outright lied! A year later, the truth came out. In 1996, they were heard on a cassette tape saying that they knew their ads enticed teens to smoke. That's why they made the ads—to get you to smoke! Former cigarette industry employees went on TV and said cigarette makers did spike cigarettes, and they did know nicotine was addictive. A year later, officials of one cigarette company *admitted* they'd been lying for years, and they settled lawsuits with several states. No matter how rich or poor or young or old you are, your lies *will* be exposed.

I tell the truth even though I may be afraid to.

August 9

Some say I was born too early and denied opportunity. Heck, I was right on time!
—Buck O'Neil, Negro League first base-man

Buck O'Neil, considered the greatest Negro League first baseman, was born in an era when blacks were barred from playing in baseball's Major Leagues simply because they were black. Yet, like many blacks, Latinos, Asians, Native Americans, European immigrants and women, Buck didn't let the circumstances nor the society he was born into limit him. You were born into a society fraught with problems and challenges. But understand that society owes you nothing! You owe it to yourself to make society work for you. Buck did. Lyle "Toni" Stone, a woman who also played in the Negro Leagues disguised as a man did! Many of you have ancestors who marched and boycotted and put their lives on the line when they wanted to change things they couldn't accept. What are you doing?

I am stepping up to life's challenges.

August 10

When you find someone who you can share your life
with, build with and love, then what difference does
it make about color. We are two people in love. I'm
black and he's white. It's that simple.
—Alfre Woodard

Sometimes, the subject of interracial dating isn't so
simple. Sometimes, your parents forbid you to date
someone outside your so-called race. Some African
American parents live with the very real fear that, in
America, black men and boys can still be killed for
being with a white girl. Other parents though, of all
so-called races don't want you dating outside your
"race" because of their prejudices. Where do these
prejudices come from? Did your parents watch you
have a bad experience while dating someone of a
different "race?" Did that lead them to think that if
one of "them" will treat you that way they all will? Is
that true? What about your own "race?" If you're
white or Chinese or black or Mexican and someone
white or Chinese or black or Mexican does you
wrong, does that mean everybody white or Chinese
or black or Mexican will do you wrong?

*I judge people as individuals, instead of stereotyping
them by their so-called race.*

August 11

You always see white people putting down black people. And you always see black people putting down white people. Racism is never going to stop because nobody knows how to respect anybody.
—Lyz Eaddy

Did you ever notice how neighbors who might not normally help each other out manage to help each other out the minute a natural disaster strikes? Your town experiences a blizzard, and suddenly, neighbors are helping each other shovel out their cars or an earthquake or a flood hits and everybody comes together to help get through the difficult times. Why is that? It's because when a blizzard hits, everybody's car and driveway and walkway is snowed in and everyone has something in common. So perhaps one way to chip away at the cylinder block of racism is to try to figure out what you have in common with someone of a different so-called race. And don't wait for an earthquake or a flood or a blizzard before you begin to discover what you have in common with someone who *appears to be* different from you.

I get to know people who, on the surface, seem to be different from me.

August 12

Salsa music is for all kinds of people. My kind of salsa is about love and it makes people happy.
—Marc Anthony

Many factors influence what kind of music you like or don't like. And most music that we think of as coming from one source actually gets its sound from several different sources. Salsa, mambo, conga, meringue and Latin jazz, for instance, are different kinds of Latin music with one thing in common—the drum! The drums that you commonly hear in the music, the tambour, the conga and the bongo, were brought to Cuba, Puerto Rico and Latin American countries by enslaved African. Other instruments, including the Spanish guitar, the accordion, the fiddle, and Native American instruments such as marimbas and maracas were added to produce the different Latin sounds. Sometimes we think certain kinds of music belong to certain groups of people. Word! There are all kinds of music out there, and what you like or don't like is your choice and your business.

It's okay for me to like whatever kind of music sounds good to me.

August 13

I grew up around jazz! I remember coming home from elementary school every day and seeing my father, a jazz drummer, listening to music or practicing or rehearsing with his band.
—Wessell Anderson

Jazz, blues, spirituals, rhythm and blues, rap and hip hop are musical forms created by African-Americans. Jazz got its start in New Orleans. Jazz is a combination of West African rhythms and European harmonies with elements of work songs, spirituals, blues songs and Latin American, West Indian and Amerindian music thrown in. Jazz greats like, Buddy Bolden, Jelly Roll Morton, Louis Armstrong, Duke Ellington, Mary Lou Williams, Mario Bauza, Sarah Vaughn, Ella Fitzgerald, Miles Davis, John Coltrane, Tony Williams and Joe Zawinul changed jazz by bringing something new to it. A new wave of jazz musicians—Roy Hargrove, Cassandra Wilson, Wynton Marsalis, Benny Green and Wessell Anderson—have made sure that jazz continues to evolve. If you haven't been exposed to jazz, go to your local library and borrow jazz CDs.

I have a rich musical heritage.

August 14

Young people need something to strive for, but they should look to all races, not one race in particular.
—Michael De Lorenzo

There are people from all "races" who can inspire and motivate you. In December 1995, just two weeks before Christmas, an explosion injured 25 people and left 3,000 Malden Mills employees without jobs. The mill's owner, Aaron Feuerstein, didn't look at the race of his employees when he decided to pay them for 90 days even though they couldn't return to work until the plant was repaired. When Rex Neilson sold his car dealership and used his own money to produce a CD with homeless men and women, he didn't just audition and select homeless people who were white like him to appear on the CD, *Voices of the Homeless.* When Sharon Draper, a black woman, was named Teacher of the Year in 1997, it wasn't because she inspired her black students only!

I look up to people who are doing good things regardless of their race.

August 15

You're not going to always win—in fact, you're going to fall down—but the main thing is to get back up.
—Mark Crear

Are you a sore loser? Do you want to quit the game the minute your team gets behind? When your team starts to lose, do you get so mad you could hit somebody? Do you have to have your way all the time? If you answered no to these questions, good! If you answered yes to these questions good—here's your chance to grow. *You will not always win and you cannot have your way all the time.* You have to compromise and you have to respect other people. Now, about losing: when you don't win, it doesn't mean you're no good. Losing doesn't make you a loser! Losing means you didn't win that time. Losing doesn't make you bad and everybody else good. Everybody loses sometimes. Of course it's natural to want to win and to dislike losing. But it's the losing you need to dislike—not yourself for losing.

Even when I lose I'm a winner because I always give my best, and I never quit.

August 16

One thing I learned is money is a false sense of security. A person that secures himself with money and fancy cars is nothing.
—Mike Tyson

Although blowing up and coming into mad money may be enable you to change things on the outside, money can't change who you are on the inside. Unfortunately, some athletes, rock stars and rappers are well aware of this. If you're the kind of person who gets off on abusing other people, running in gangs or abusing drugs, all the money in the world won't take away your desire to do these things. If you have problems now controlling your temper or treating others with respect, those problems don't magically disappear when you become wealthy. Money is not the answer to all your problems. Like Mike says, you're fooling yourself if you think having lots of money will give you a sense of security. Money can buy you cars, clothes and concert tickets, but it can't make you feel secure. It can't make you feel good about you, love you or believe in you.

I believe in myself. I am good enough.

Niggas that wasn't shit and I knew it used to dis me. But I didn't have no money and that's what used to fuck me up. It be shitty dumb niggas who had women, rides, houses and I ain't have shit.
—Tupac Shakur

If you can put aside Tupac's bad, offensive language and understand what he's saying, you'll probably realize you've felt the same way at times. Tupac and his mother moved around a lot during his childhood. He never really got to know his father who died of a crack-induced heart attack at 41. As a teen, Tupac, like many of us, thought that having money, women, rides and houses would give him a sense that he was somebody and a sense that he special. But if you don't know you're somebody special before you get money, women, rides or houses, you won't know after you get those things. Oh sure, you'll get off on your new possessions. But if the outside changes and the inside stays the same, you'll eventually feel the same. You still won't feel loved and important and valued. You still won't have a sense of self-worth.

My self-worth comes from who I am on the inside, not what I have on the outside.

August 18

I don't have time to hate anyone because when you sit here and hate someone, that's a burden on your heart. That's a stress.

—Prakazrel Michel of the Fugees

Where does hatred come from? People who hate others hate themselves! White supremacists, Skinheads and anyone who hates somebody because they're black or white or Asian or Puerto Rican or gay or rich or poor or whatever, is someone who hates himself. And people who hate themselves are afraid. They're not afraid of other people, but they're afraid they're no good. They're afraid no one loves them, and they're afraid they don't matter. Because they can't admit to themselves they don't matter, they take their hatred for themselves and put it on others. And they can only do that when they believe all the lies they've heard about others. You know, lies that say "They're all like that!" or "We're better than them!" Word! You can get rid of your hatred for others by getting rid of your hatred for yourself!

I am learning how to love myself and how to love others.

August 19

I have crossed over the backs of Sojourner Truth, Harriet Tubman, Fannie Lou Hamer and Madame C.J. Walker. Because of them I can now live the dream.

—Oprah Winfrey

Sojourner Truth and Harriet Tubman helped enslaved people get their freedom. Madame C.J. Walker was a successful businesswoman who gave back to her Harlem community. Fannie Lou Hamer, the daughter of sharecroppers, became a civil rights activist. Without brave men and women—African-Americans, whites, Latinos, Asians and Native Americans—you wouldn't enjoy many of the freedoms you have today. Back in the day, it was against the law to teach black people to read. Back in the day, blacks and Latinos were denied the right to vote. And, until 1920, women couldn't vote! No, things are not perfect now, but they're a lot better than they were. It's time to stop making excuses for why you can't accomplish what you want. Too many people have paved the way for you to make excuses and to give up on your dreams!

I can live my dreams!

August 20

Everybody has a way to get to college. You study in high school, you do your work. There are always grants or loans that can be available.
　　　　　—Muggsy Bogues

You *can* get money for college! Go to your library, pick up *The Higher Education MoneyBook for Minorities and Women* or *The Scholarship Book* and get that money! Listed below are a few scholarship and funding sources to contact:

The National Hispanic Scholarship Fund P.O. Box 728, Novato, CA 94948. Ph: (415) 892-9971; Fax (415) 898-6673.
Cesar Chavez Memorial Leadership Award $2,500 for candidates who've displayed outstanding leadership both academically and in the community. Write to: TELACU Education Foundation, 5400 E. Olympic Blvd., Suite 300, Los Angeles, CA 90022.
Thurgood Marshall Scholarship Fund $16,000 over a four-year period for students attending an Historically Black College or University. Write to: The Thurgood Marshall Scholarship Fund; 100 Park Avenue, 10th Fl.; New York, NY 10017

I can get money for school!

August 21

You'll find that many scholarships aren't for the top academic people. Just regular *C* and *C-plus* students can also obtain some of this money.
—Dr. William Young

U.S. Institute of Peace. 1550 M. St. NW; Suite 700, Washington, DC 20005 (202) 457-1700. 1500-word essay contest for scholarships for American history and foreign policy majors. Open to 9th- through 12th-graders. 166 state winners. Three national winners.

Chicana Latina Foundation Scholarships. Must have a minimum 2.5 grade point average. PO Box 27083, Oakland, CA 94602 Phone: (510) 869-3588.

Air Force AID Society. 1745 Jefferson Davis Hwy #202; Arlington, VA 22202; 800-429-9475. $1000 scholarships for undergrads in all fields who are dependent children of active duty, retired or deceased members of the Air Force. Must maintain 2.0 GPA.

National Association of Black Journalists. Print, radio and TV, and photojournalism scholarships. Must have at least a 2.5 GPA. Write to: NABJ; 3100 Taliaferro Hall; University of Maryland; College Park, MD 20742-7717; Ph: (301) 405-8500; Fax (301)405-8555; e-mail: nabj@jmail.umd.edu.

Nothing will stop me from going to college.

August 22

I think my parents did some miracle work. They raised 10 kids in the projects and none of us are dead or in jail.

—Marlon Wayans

Today is parents', grandparents', stepparents' and foster parents' appreciation day! No matter where they live, in the inner city or the suburbs, parents have a tough job raising their children. And having to raise teenagers is almost as tough as being a teenager! So why not take time out today to tell whomever takes care of you how much you appreciate what they've done for you. If you're not speaking to your parents or if you're mad at them, think about all the good things they've done for you. Then think about the fact that they'll still be doing good things for you even after you're grown and gone from home. Perhaps, when you look at it that way, you'll decide it makes sense to let go of your anger and take some time out to give your parents their props!

I appreciate my parents!

August 23

If you don't know where you're going you're already
there.

—Antonia Novello

Where are you going right now? A year from now?
To school? Work? To cheerleading practice? To
make some paper? Dance class? Home? College?
The youth center? To put a cap in somebody? To get
some skins? How will you get there? No matter
where you go in life, you need a plan to get there. If
you want to go to college or get a good job when you
finish high school, you have to plan for that now. If
you want to make your high school baseball, soccer
or IQ team, you have to plan for that now. If selling
drugs, running with a gang or getting pregnant will
mess up your plan, then you have to choose not to do
those things. "But if I don't join a gang, I'll get my ass
kicked." "I need to sell drugs to help my moms out
with money." Those are excuses. Excuses will not get
you to college, to a starting spot on the football team
or hired by the company you want to work for.

I am in control of my future.

August 24

If you are building a house and the nail breaks, do you stop building or do you change the nail?
—Rwanda Burindi Proverb

Life is filled with setbacks. Why? *It just is.* Nothing in life is perfect. Things will not go the way you want them to all the time. When things don't go your way, do you cry about it? Do you scream out that life sucks? Do you say, "Life isn't fair"? If you do, you're not alone! But instead of getting upset and trying to figure out if something is fair or unfair, figure out what you can learn from it. Life may suck for a minute, an hour, even for a day. Just remember, when life sucks, life is giving you a chance to become a better person. Every problem, every setback, every obstacle you face in life is really an opportunity for you to grow and to become a stronger, more mature person.

As I overcome life's challenges, I become a better me.

August 25

What part of no don't you understand?
—Common Saying

How happy do you think you'd be if you got everything you ever wanted in life? How good do you think your life would be if you never faced rejection? Rejection sucks! It's embarrassing! But rejection has a good side too! Rejection can save you from things that are no good for you. Rejection has another upside. You see, you don't have to worry about how happy you'd be if you always got everything you wanted in life because you never will. Life doesn't work that way. So rejection keeps you down to earth! If you never got rejected, you might actually start believing you can get anything you want. People who think that way often end up in trouble. They break laws and hurt others because they think they can have anyone they want, do anything they want and get away with everything. Wrong! You see, rejection can actually be good for you!

Things don't always go the way I'd like them to and that's okay.

August 26

Most of my songs started from the time that my parents separated. It was a very painful time in my life. It felt like my father walked out on me. I took everything so personally.

—Casserine

People don't get married with the intention of getting divorced and suffering through the pain that goes with most divorces. If your parents are going through a separation or divorce, you may fault one over the other. That's understandable. You may even blame yourself. That's also understandable. But no matter what may have happened, you're not the reason your parents are getting divorced or separated. Like Casserine, it's normal to feel like one of your parents is abandoning you when they get divorced. It's also normal to feel sick inside or to cry a lot. If you feel sick and cry, it's usually because you're depressed and angry about the divorce. There's no magic pill to take to keep from feeling anger or guilt or to keep from feeling like your father or mother walked out on you. Remember, divorce is hard on everyone and it may take some time for you to get over it.

My parents' divorce is painful, but I'm learning how to deal with it.

August 27

We ate a lot of bologna sandwiches.
—John B. McLendon Jr.

Back in the day, some basketball players missed out on a lot more than large commercial endorsements and FootLocker shoe stores. When John McLendon coached for the North Carolina College for Negroes (now A & T State University) his players couldn't eat in the same restaurants or stay in the same hotels as whites. If there wasn't a black-owned hotel for McLendon's team to stay in, the team ate and slept on the bus. Blacks, Latinos, Native Americans, Asians, women and other minority groups are still discriminated against. Yes, discrimination hurts! So, it's up to *you* to continue the fight against discrimination, racism, sexism and homophobia. Your parents, grandparents and great-grandparents did their part, so that today, African-Americans don't have to sit in their cars and eat bologna sandwiches. It's your turn to make things better for the next generation.

I'm doing my part.

August 28

You probably always learn a lot more when you lose than when you win.

—Venus Williams

You're not going to win all the time. Nobody does. You'll never achieve everything you set out to achieve in life. Nobody has. The key to living a successful life, though, is how you deal with your wins and your losses. When you win or succeed, you need to know why you succeeded. Then, you'll understand what works for you and where your strengths are. When you lose or fail, you also need to figure out why you failed. And like Venus says, you'll probably learn more from examining your losses than from feeling good about your wins. Losing or failing is not the end of the world, it just means you have something more to learn. When you lose, don't give up, try again *but try a different strategy!* And remember, losing doesn't make you a loser. Everybody loses sometimes! The question is, will you learn from your losses?

I am learning how to succeed.

August 29

It's painful to see what America has done to the black family, painful to see what we've done to ourselves. We need to watch each other's backs.
—Babyface

There's enough blame to go around for why things aren't as good as they could be for blacks, Latinos and Asians in America. But how many of your problems have you solved by blaming someone else? None! *Cero*! Not one! It's time to accept whatever situation you find yourself in and move forward, not backward. If things are going good for you right now—great! Be thankful for your situation. If things aren't going the way you want them, and if life is painful for you right now, accept your life, and make up your mind that things will get better. Don't blame your mom, dad, aunt, uncle, teachers, coach, society, racism or the past for what's going on with you. Forgive whomever you need to for whatever happened! Let the past go and move forward. You can't watch your brother's or your sister's back until you learn to take care of your own.

My life is in my hands!

I was from the projects; that was all I knew. I was loud; I didn't know how to be polite. And I thought he couldn't stand me because of that. So to make him stand me, I tried to better myself.
—Wanya Morris of Boyz II Men

Some neighborhoods are said to be bad, others good. In a so-called bad neighborhood, if only a few people are bad, the entire neighborhood gets a reputation for being bad. But all people from the projects aren't bad. And all people from so-called good neighborhoods don't always do the right things. Wherever you grow up, you can choose to act like the people around you or you can choose not to. Sometimes, behavior that's cool in your neighborhood or on the streets, may not be cool in school or in other public places. It's okay, like Wanya, to want to change your behavior. It's also okay to change your behavior and still be proud of where you come from! Remember, you can dislike some things about yourself, but still love yourself while you work to change those things you don't like.

I approve of myself and the way I am changing.

August 31

I don't believe in I can't. *I can* do whatever I want, and I'm going to.

—Lez

Some people think that people living in housing projects can't make it in life. They're wrong! No matter where you live or where you have lived, you can make it! Weequaic Towers! Dayton Street! Miller Homes! You *Can* Make It! Cabrini-Green! Robert Taylor! King-Kennedy Estates! You *Can* Too! Few Gardens! Ray Warren! Walnut Terrace! Yes You *Can!* Richard Allen Homes! Peter J. McGuire Gardens! Don't Let Anyone Tell You You Can't Make It! Murphy Homes! Barry Farms! Potomac Gardens! You Know You *Can* Make It! Orchard Park! Academy Homes! Charter Oak Terrace! You *Can* Too! Highbridge Houses! Red Hook Houses! Mott Haven! Yes You *Can!* Bankhead Court! Perry Homes! Smiley Court! Don't Let Anyone Tell You You Can't Make It! *Wherever You Are, Don't Let Anybody Tell You Can't, Because You Can!*

I know I can make it!

If you love me you'll . . .

September 1

Sometimes you may see somebody and you may wanna have sex with 'em because they turn you on. That's the reality of life. And then you can love someone and want to have sex with them because you love 'em.

—R. Kelly

Teenagers' answers to the question, "Why did you first have sex?" I really didn't want to, but I wanted to know how it felt. • I felt like I had to because his friends, they were all doing it, and if they're doing it, I had to do it. • I was curious. I did it on my own. I wasn't peer-pressured or anything. • All my friends would talk about that it hurt and stuff, and I just wanted to see how it felt. • 'Cause I didn't want to let my friends keep thinking that I ain't had none. • I thought it was my first love, and it was actually my first dog! • You have to do it. Once you're at this age group, forget it, everybody just laughs at you. • I would hang around people that always would talk about that, always, and I would think about it and wonder how it is. But if people wouldn't sweat that so much, I wouldn't even care about it.

I overcome peer pressure when deciding whether or not to have sex.

September 2

The greatest responsibility I feel is to my creator, and
what I try to fulfill for myself is to honor the creation.
—Oprah Winfrey.

The power that created everything created you. That
power, call it God, call it the Creator, call it whatever
it is for you, lives inside you. When you honor the
Creator's creation, you honor you! When you honor
the Creator's creation, you honor life—your life, your
parents' lives, strangers' lives, everyone's life. You
don't honor your life by abusing it. And when you
abuse sex, you abuse your life, you abuse your spirit,
you abuse you. You don't honor you by throwing
open your legs to any boy who asks. You don't honor
you by trying to get with as many girls as you can.
You don't honor you by giving into peer pressure and
having sex. You weren't created to screw as many
women as you can count. You weren't created to give
it up to as many cute boys as you can find. You are a
spiritual creation living in a physical body, and you
were created for something special.

I honor who I am.

September 3

I don't treat women like shit because I don't want to see women treated like shit, and I try to learn from women how not to treat them like shit because I don't think anyone teaches us how.
—Bill T. Jones

Some of you have wonderful role models teaching you how to treat women—your fathers and grandfathers. Some of you have a father who treats his wife with respect and love. If you've learned to love you, accept you and value you, you can love, accept and value others. It gets back to doing unto others as you would have them do unto you! Women nor men, girls nor boys are sex objects! Girls are not pieces of meat just waiting for you guys to come along and make them feel pleasure for a few minutes. Girls have bodies—bodies that are attractive to you—but girls also have minds and spirits. Girls weren't put on this earth just so you boys could snap their bras and feel on them in school and have sex with them whenever you want to.

I treat girls the way they deserve to be treated—with respect and love.

September 4

Women need to realize that sex is supposed to be something special.
—Chilli of TLC

What's the purpose of sex in a relationship? Sex allows two people to grow closer to each other. It's called being intimate. Sex allows adults to gain greater intimacy. But sex is not the only way two mature people become intimate. Intimacy is also achieved by talking, hanging out and sharing each other's space. And true intimacy can take several years to develop. You don't become intimate with someone by having sex with them two weeks or even two months after you start dating them. The sex act is a spiritual act as much as it is a physical act when enjoyed by two people taking care of each other's spirits. If you're having sex as a teenager, and you're not in an intimate relationship where you're committed to taking care of your partner's spirit, then you're abusing sex. Sex has a purpose. Like Chilli said, sex is supposed to be something special.

I treat sex like it's something special.

September 5

I went through a phase where I was bisexual because to me that was more acceptable. I could still say, 'Hey, I want her!'—when you know I didn't.
—Wilson Cruz

As a teenager sometimes the hardest thing to be is yourself. There are many reasons why you pretend to be someone you're not. One is the fear you won't be accepted and liked if people know the real you. If you're gay, you may not feel accepted by other kids. It's true some kids won't accept you because they think there's something wrong with you if you're gay or lesbian. So now what? Will you pretend to be someone you're not just to be accepted. Will you hide who you really are because you're afraid your friends wouldn't be your friends if they knew you were gay? Will you hide who you are for fear you'd be beaten up if the wrong people found out? Always be true to yourself. Always be who you are and be proud of who you are. People who try to deny who they are and people who don't accept themselves as they are are miserable people.

I love and approve of myself.

September 6

Young people have to start loving themselves more.
Not conceited or selfish love, but real, true love—
that's what it's about.
                    —Diana King

Yes, being in love feels great. But, what exactly is
love? Is love selfish? Is love demanding? Is love
abusive, as in, "Baby I love you, and if I see you even
talking to another guy, I'll knock your teeth out?"
No, love is not selfish, demanding, jealous, abusive
or anything negative. Love is a powerful force at the
center of your spirit, and love is what holds you
together. When you love yourself, you're patient with
yourself and you don't demand that you be perfect.
When you love you, you accept both the good and
bad parts of your personality and you figure out how
to change those things about you that could use some
changing. The same applies when you love others—
you're patient with them, you accept both their good
and their bad and you give them space to grow. All
that other crap—selfishness, jealousy, wanting
someone to be what you want them to be—is not
love!

My love is patient and accepting.

September 7

This thing is real and it doesn't discriminate. It affects everyone.

— Eazy-E

Rap star, Eazy-E, died from AIDS. AIDS is caused by HIV, one of many sexually transmitted diseases affecting teenagers. Diseases like gonorrhea, syphilis and chlamydia are curable. HIV is not. It would be nice if all the people in charge of hiring were always as fair as HIV. Some people who make hiring decisions sometimes, hire or don't hire people because of their skin color. But HIV doesn't care if you're black, brown, yellow, red, white or polka-dotted! HIV doesn't discriminate when deciding whom to infect. HIV is a viral infection transmitted through your bloodstream. HIV is transmitted through semen and vaginal secretions present during oral, vaginal and anal sex. HIV is also transmitted by sharing heroin and crack needles with HIV-infected blood on them. HIV has also been transmitted through blood transfusions. HIV doesn't discriminate! HIV doesn't care! Do you?

I care about staying healthy and free of sexually transmitted diseases.

September 8

Making love is more than sex. It's hugging, holding hands and so much more than what you hear on the radio.
> —Tony Terry

Having sex can be about bumpin', grindin', slappin' it, flippin' it and rubbin' it down. But, like Tony says, making love is about so much more. It takes mature people to understand the beauty and the power of making love. Making love *is* holding hands, hugging and caressing each other's bodies. Making love is also a spiritual act when shared by two people taking care of each others spirits. How do you take care of someone's spirit? You treat them right. You revere them. You don't try to change them, rather you accept them. You help them reach their dreams by encouraging them. You value them. You appreciate them. You do all these things and then some. It takes a mature person to know how to take care of his own and someone else's spirit. If you're not a mature person, *then making love is not for you—yet!*

Making love is a spiritual act when shared by two people taking care of each others spirits.

September 9

My mom told me to open doors for girls and pull out their chairs. I never understood why until I started doing it and noticed that it made them feel nice.
                    —Shawn Stockman of Boyz II Men

Instead of walking up to girls and asking them, "So when you gonna sex me?" or "When you gonna let me getwhichu?" why not try respecting the ladies for a change. Why not walk up to a girl and say, "Allow me to open the door for you." And after you've opened the door for her, don't expect anything other than a "thank you" in return! It doesn't always have to be about gettin' wit' somebody. You may think it does, but it doesn't. Your life is about far more than gettin' some skins. And girls' lives are about much more than letting you hit it! Girls want to be respected. They don't want to be used and abused by boys. Sure some girls don't respect themselves. But just because a girl doesn't respect herself is no reason for you to try to get over. Just because a girl hasn't figured out the meaning of self respect, is no reason for you to dog her.

I respect women even if they don't respect themselves.

September 10

Song No. 2 by Sonia Sanchez—*Under A Soprano Sky*

i say. all you young girls waiting to live
i say. all you young girls taking yo pill
i say. all you sisters tired of standing still
i say. all you sisters thinkin you won't, but you will.
    don't let them kill with their stare
    don't let them closet you with no air
    don't let them feed you sex piece-meal
    don't let them offer you any old deal.
i say. step back sisters. we're rising from the dead
i say. step back johnnies. we're dancing on our heads
i say. step back man. no mo hangin by a thread
i say. step back world. can't let it all go unsaid.
i say. all you young girls molested at ten
i say. all you young girls giving it up again & again
i say. all you sisters hanging out in every den
i say. all you sisters needing your own oxygen.
    don't let them trap you with their coke
    don't let them treat you like one fat joke
    don't let them bleed you till you broke
    don't let them blind you in masculine smoke.
i say. step back sisters. we're rising from the dead
i say. step back johnnies. we're dancing on our heads
i say. step back man. no mo hanging by a thread
i say. step back world. can't let it go unsaid.

September 11

When the cock is drunk, he forgets about the hawk.
—Ashanti proverb

How many smart things do you do when you're drunk off a 40? How straight are you thinking after you've smoked mad weed? Sometimes, when you're faded you forget about syphilis, gonorrhea, chlamydia, herpes, crabs, genital warts and HIV. You may forget about syphilis, gonorrhea, chlamydia, herpes, crabs, genital warts and HIV when you're high, but these living, breathing viruses, bacteria and microbes don't forget about you! Wear a condom if you have sex! Condoms are not a 100 percent guarantee against contracting sexually transmitted diseases, but they can reduce the odds!

I always protect myself against sexually transmitted diseases.

September 12

It's super, super hard. You have no social life. You lose your friends, one by one. Everyone knows you won't be able to do anything. Sometimes you get lonely.

—Michelle Beltran

Michelle got pregnant and had a baby. Some girls think a baby will give them the love they're not getting from parents. Others think having a baby will trap their boyfriend into staying with them or get them out of a bad home and living with their boyfriend. Still others want the attention girls get from teachers and others when they're pregnant. As Michelle says, being a teenage mother is super hard so let's understand it better. Your baby will *not* be able to give you the love you've been missing from your parents. Your baby needs *your* love, just like you need your parents' love! Getting pregnant and having a baby is *not* a good way to keep a man nor is it a good way to escape a bad home. And wanting attention is perfectly normal. But once your baby's born, things change and you may not get the same kind or the same of attention as before.

I am finding constructive ways to get the love and attention I need.

September 13

It's been hard because I'm so used to getting what I wanted. Now I have to wait two weeks to get what I want because I never know what my daughter's going to need.

—Lyz Eaddy

Not all girls who get pregnant want to. Maybe you were on the pill but missed a few, or maybe your partner was using a condom but it broke or maybe you didn't use protection and now regret it. The good news is that many of you who become teenage mothers get help from your school and other places and you're doing a great job caring for your children. You understand you have to do things differently now that you have a baby depending on you. Instead of dropping out of school, you stay in school. Those of you who continue with school often have the support of your parents and grandparents who help you out financially and in many other ways. And just like Lyz Eaddy, you understand that even though you're still kids, you have to act like mature adults because your child's needs have to come before your own. It's not easy, but you're doing a great job!

I am a good teenage mother.

September 14

The whole notion that fathers cannot be as loving and nurturing as mothers is bogus and chauvinistic. As women and mothers, we should be overjoyed with a father's involvement with his children.
—Alfre Woodard

Congratulations! You're a teenage father, and, as hard as it is, you're doing a great job with your kid. You understand that as your infant grows into a toddler, she's struggling to become independent. And you know she gets frustrated because she can't tell you everything she's feeling and she sometimes throws tantrums. But instead of spanking her when she has a fit, you hold her gently and talk to her about why she's upset. You also know your child likes to imitate you, and when you're outside working on your car, your son is out there with you working on the toy car you bought him. You're also reading to him! You know that because you're reading to him, he's talking at an earlier age, and he's developing his mind and his creativity. Congratulations dad! You're doing a great job taking care of your kid!

I'm doing a great job loving and raising my child!

September 15

For six years of my life, he raped me constantly. I felt like trash.

—Anna Maria Nieves founder of
Urban X, a youth advocacy group

Unfortunately, some promiscuous teenage girls have been sexually abused. If you've been sexually abused by your father, uncle, brother, grandfather, stepfather, cousin, your mother's boyfriend, or by a stranger, your self-esteem has been shattered. Sexual abuse can make you feel as though you have no control over what happens to you or to your body. And some girls who've been abused have a hard time saying no. You may even end up in a relationship with an older man because he seems to give you the attention, and romance you need. You think because he's older, he'll be responsible and take care of you if you get pregnant. But most men mess with teenage girls because teenagers don't expect as much from them as adult women do. *They're using you.* If you've been sexually abused, talk to a therapist who can help you understand how the to get beyond the abuse.

I am learning how to heal from a painful past.

September 16

My family expects me to be something big.
—Robert Rodriguez

What are your family's expectations for you. Do you hear things like "You can be anything you want in life!" or "You have a great future ahead of you!" Or, have you heard things like, "You're not going to amount to nothing," or "You'll be dead by the time you're eighteen." If you haven't yet realized it, realize it now—*you get out of life exactly what you expect!* If your parents have been encouraging and supportive and loving, don't turn your back on their love, their support and their encouragement. You are going to make it and make it big! If your parents have given up on you, don't you give up on you! You can amount to something! You can be anything you want in life! What do you want to be? Who do you want to be like? Do you want a good, happy, meaningful life? Then start believing you can have one.

I have big plans for my life!

September 17

Not how many women I can get, not how many cars
or how many houses or whatever. That's not what's
important. What's important is how do we make the
world a better place.
—Malik Yoba

Back in the 50s, 60s and 70s, many Latinos and
African-Americans helped make the world better by
fighting for school integration, boycotting for better
treatment of farm workers and demanding an end to
housing and employment discrimination. So how do
you make the world a better place now? By becoming
the best possible you you can become. You don't
need lots of money to become the best possible you.
All you need is *ganas*, desire! And as you mature,
you'll find out what your special contribution to the
world will be. You'll never discover your mission,
though, if you don't feel good about who you are.
And you have to feel good about you whether you
have men, women, cars, houses—whatever. These
things don't make you somebody. You're somebody
if you don't have them, and if you do have them, you
were somebody before you got them.

I'm doing my part to help make the world better.

September 18

I guess no matter how "large" you get, to your parents you're still children with lessons to learn.
—Jojo

Even rap and rock stars have to obey their parents! Just ask Jojo! Remember, you were put on earth for a reason. And you came to the planet to learn some lessons. There are things you're supposed to accomplish while you're alive, and there are lessons you have to learn in order to accomplish those things. Your parents are here to help you learn your lessons. No, your parents don't have all the answers. Nobody does. No, your parents aren't perfect. Nobody is. Yes, parents make mistakes too. Everybody does. But there's nothing wrong with making mistakes. Mistakes teach people what not to do in the future. Remember, your parents want to help you, and you're never too old to learn from your parents. When you become a teenager, that's not the time to start dissin' and ignoring your parents. That's the time when you need your parents' guidance and help the most.

When I accept my parents' guidance, I accept my parents' love.

September 19

I thought, 'God, I'm not perfect. I'm going to disappoint people.' That's what I thought."
—Paula Abdul

No one is perfect. And no one has a perfect body. Unfortunately, the images shown on television and in the movies can make you believe there is a perfect body. When you believe you're nothing and nobody if you don't look like the people in music videos, you're setting yourself up to fail. How? You're basing your self-worth and your self-esteem on how you look. But looks don't really mean what you think they do. Just because someone is fine or handsome doesn't mean they're a good person or a smart person. You can't know what kind of person someone is by how they look. You need to feel good about yourself no matter how you look! And you need to stop thinking that the best-looking people are the smartest or the happiest or the ones having the most fun. Your looks don't make you who you are. Your thoughts and your actions make you who you are.

My self-worth comes from inside me and it's not based only on my looks.

September 20

Kids made fun of me because I was dark-skinned, had a wide nose and was tall and skinny.
—Danny Glover

Kids make fun of other kids. And when someone makes fun of you, it usually hurts. Sometimes, the kids making fun of you have their own problems and they're trying to make themselves feel better by ragging on you. Still, even though everybody may laugh, the person making fun of you doesn't feel better after the laughing stops. What was wrong with them before they made fun of you is wrong with them afterward. You've read much in this book about loving who you are and embracing your ancestry and being proud of where you come from. If someone decides they want to make fun of your facial features or the way you talk or how dark or light you are, that's on them. It's on you to be proud of your skin color and your facial features. Your creator and your parents gave you those things and you shouldn't let anybody make you feel bad about them.

My nose is my nose! My lips are my lips. My color is my color, and I am beautiful!

September 21

Basically I kind of felt like I had an empty hole after my mother died. The only thing I had to comfort me was food.

—Zina Garrison-Jackson

Zina, a professional tennis player, lost several close family members as a teenager and young adult. After her mother died in 1983, she dealt with the tragedy by stuffing herself with food. After binging on food, she would feel guilty and make herself throw up. The condition she suffered from is an eating disorder called bulimia. It usually strikes young women who have undergone a traumatic experience or a major life change. With bulimia, food is used the same as drugs are used—to try to make you forget about your pain. Zina got help for her eating disorder by talking with a therapist. In addition to dealing with the death of her mother, the therapist helped Zina understand she was an okay person. When you begin to feel okay about you, you begin to feel more secure. When you're secure and feeling worthwhile, you're better able to handle life's traumatic events when they happen.

I love and approve of myself.

September 22

The time of begging somebody to put on a condom is getting old.
—Jasmine Guy

If you're a teenage girl and you're having sex, you may be having sex with a guy older than you. No matter how young or how old your sex partner is, he needs to wear a condom to reduce his risk and yours of contracting HIV, syphilis, gonorrhea, chlamydia, herpes, crabs or genital warts. Condoms are not a 100 percent guarantee against contracting a sexually transmitted disease, but they can reduce the odds! If your partner is older than you, you may feel intimidated by him. You may be afraid to even mention the word *condom* to him. It's normal to be intimidated by someone older and more experienced than you. If you're messing with someone who intimidates you, maybe you should find someone who doesn't. If you prefer hanging out with older guys because they're more mature, then you need to learn how to tell your older guy to wear a condom.

I have the courage to tell my boyfriend to use condoms.

September 23

The bottom line is family is all we really have. Your family background is the stabilizing force in your life.
—Steve Harvey

Family should be the stabilizing force in your life, but sometimes it isn't. Some parents don't get along and they split up. Other parents have difficulties, but their love and their commitment to their marriage help them get through the rough times. If you're living with your mother and her boyfriend that can be tough, especially if you and her boyfriend don't get along. You may feel as though your mom takes his side when you try to talk with her about your problems with him. Your parents may be divorced and you may be living with a stepparent. None of these situations is easy. And you may wish you didn't have to deal with stepparents, your parent's boyfriend or girlfriend or even your own parents! If you're in a difficult family situation, don't give up. Why? Because if things are bad, that means they can always get better!

My family may not be perfect, but I deal with my family situation the best I can.

September 24

You have to bring a child into the world first, but that's just the beginning. It's like a plant. When it grows, you have to take care of it. That's what responsibility is.

—Shaquille O'Neal

Some of you have fathers who have abandoned their responsibility. Some fathers bring children into the world, but don't hang around to watch them grow. Shaquille O'Neal's father left him and his mother when Shaq was a baby. Fortunately for Shaq, he was reared by a loving, supportive and responsible stepfather. If your father isn't around, you're probably angry and confused about why he left. You probably wish he'd come back and be responsible and be a man and be there for you when you need him. Well, it may happen and it may never happen. If your father isn't there for you, get angry if you have to. But never, never, ever think there's something wrong with you because your father didn't stick around to be responsible for you. Never think your father left because of you or something you did or didn't do. It wasn't your fault. *You are not the problem!*

I'm a great kid who deserves all the love I can get!

September 25

It's hectic. You have your own things to take care of. When you have a baby, you also have to look out for its needs. You have to remember diapers, remember your schoolbooks, make the formula.
—Melissa Cosme

If you're a teenage mother who's decided to stay in school, your life won't be easy, and you'll definitely need some support! If your baby cries a lot, he or she could have colic. Colic is normal in babies and usually goes away when your baby is around 3 months old. No matter how much your baby cries, never shake it! Babies' necks aren't strong enough to support their still-developing heads and brains, and if you shake them, you can damage their brains and even kill them. If you get the urge to shake your baby because you're angry and overwhelmed, don't. Don't take out your frustrations on your baby! Instead, take a break and get a relative to care for your baby until you're no longer feeling overwhelmed, frustrated and angry. When you see your baby again, give it lots of hugs and soft, gentle touches. Your baby will feel great, and so will you!

I'm working hard to be a good mother and a good student.

September 26

It takes a lot of energy to raise children.
—Andy Garcia

It takes a lot more time and energy to pull your child aside in the grocery store and explain to him why he can't go to the toy store next door than it does to slap him, grab him and drag him through the grocery store. Slapping, grabbing and dragging him through the store may allow you to release your anger, but it doesn't help him much. Letting go of your anger so you can talk rationally with him requires time, patience and positive energy—and it's a lot harder than knocking him upside the head. So why choose the harder way? Because when you calmly but firmly explain to your child why he can't have or can't do something, you teach your child a valuable lesson. And when you teach young children lessons, they learn them! When you teach your child why he can't have his way, and why what he did was wrong, he learns not to expect to have his way and he learns not to repeat his wrongs.

I am patient with my children as I teach them life's important lessons.

September 27

I got hit so hard by one of my boyfriends, he broke the eardrum in my left ear. I have no hearing there.
—Halle Berry

If your boyfriend or girlfriend is abusing you physically or sexually, you can get help. If your girlfriend or boyfriend is abusing you emotionally, you can also get help. It's easy to spot physical abuse, but if your partner humiliates you in front of your friends, tells you you're no good, curses at you or threatens you, you're being emotionally abused. If your partner threatens to kill themselves if you break up with them, they're trying to manipulate you and that's also emotional abuse. If your boyfriend tells you how to dress, who to talk to or where to go, that's another form of emotional abuse. If your partner keeps you from seeing your friends, you're being controlled and abused. If you want out of an abusive relationship, get help! Start by talking to your parents or school counselor.

I am a good person who deserves to be in a good, healthy relationship.

September 28

Sometimes, people mistake being humble for being scared, but it's much closer to being self-assured. If you're self-assured you don't have to wear your masculinity on your sleeve.
—Nathan McCall

Humble? Scared? Self-assured? Most teenage boys don't have time for such sissy words. You think you have to be hard to get your respect. And some of you end up in jail! One of the hardest brothers to ever live went to jail 39 times. *And he did not fear any man!* He was a smart brother and people feared him. They respected him too. Most guys trying to be hard get people to fear them, but they rarely gain people's respect. Well, this brother got both, and he also got gunned down. Those who were most afraid of him and angry with him paid to have him assassinated. But this brother never even used a gun to get his respect. And he didn't bully people around or even want people to fear him. His name? The Rev. Dr. Martin Luther King, Jr.!

I prove my manhood and gain my respect by being confident in myself and by doing what's right.

September 29

I don't think that disrespecting women is right.
—Speech

If you think your girlfriend is good for only giving you money, you're not giving her respect. If the only thing you want from your girlfriend is sex, you're disrespecting her. If you force your girlfriend to kiss you when she doesn't want to, wear clothes she doesn't want to or have sex when she doesn't want to, you're disrespecting her and you're abusing her. Forcing sex on her is raping her and it's a crime! And yes, it's rape even if she is your girlfriend. If you're in a relationship and you're abusing your girl, you need help. How do you know if you're abusing her? Ask yourself: Do I get jealous or overprotective? Do I have a violent temper? Do I think guys rule in a relationship? Do I try to control how she acts, who she hangs with, what she wears, where she goes? If you answer yes to any of these questions, you're abusing your girl and you need help. Start by talking things over with your parents or school counselor.

I show my girlfriend love by treating her with respect.

September 30

Most people live in dysfunctional relationships and they accept that, but I like to keep it real, and if it's not working, then I move on.
—Erika Alexander

It's not always easy to break up with your boyfriend or your girlfriend but sometimes, it's necessary. Guys, if a girl doesn't want to be with you anymore, you have to let her go. Once you've accepted that she's gone, it's time to get over her. It's hard, but it has to happen sometime. Ladies, you may not want to break up with your boyfriend, but if you're miserable in the relationship, and if you two are arguing all the time, breaking up is probably the best thing for both of you. If you're tempted to stay in a relationship that isn't working because you think you can change your boyfriend or girlfriend, remember, the only person you can change is yourself. If you don't think you have the right to break up with someone for whatever reason you want, think again. You may feel bad because you think you're hurting them, but you have to realize that you're not responsible for other people's feelings.

I have the right to end a relationship.

October 1

I don't care what the relationship is with the mother, that makes no difference. You have got to take care of the children.

—Sinbad

It doesn't matter if it happened when you were drunk. It doesn't matter if it happened when you were messin' around on your girl. It doesn't matter whether you did or didn't want it to happen. If you got a girl pregnant and she gave birth to your child, the circumstances don't really matter. If you now can't stand the girl who had your baby or if she's messin' with someone else, it still doesn't matter. And if you wanted her to have an abortion and she didn't, there's still a child in the world you helped create. Your baby is your baby no matter what, and like Sinbad says, "You have got to take care of the children." Anyone, boy or girl, who's grown up without their father's love and attention knows how painful that is. If you're now a teenage father, you have to understand how painful it will be for your child if you don't love it and protect it and take care of it.

I take care of my child.

October 2

Your children need your presence more than your presents.

—Jesse Jackson

Teenage parents, your children need you! They need for you to talk to them, not yell at them. You know how you feel when you get yelled at, don't you? Your children need your hugs and your love. They need your love just like you need and want your parents' love. Your role as a parent is to love, protect and nurture your child. When you nurture them, you're preparing them to become responsible adults. It's not easy being a teenage parent, and you won't do everything perfectly, but there are some things you can do better! *Show* your child how much you love him. Hug your child! Pick her up and hold her tight. If you give your child 10 hugs during the week, he'll feel 100 times better and be 1,000 times better off than if you give him 10 toys in a week!

I give my child love and hugs!

October 3

We're not telling kids to have sex. We're saying if you're having sex, have safe sex.
— T-Boz of TLC

Some of you can kick it with your parents about sex, others of you can't. Sometimes, parents aren't comfortable talking with you about sex. But if you are having sex, you're not just having sex—you're also putting yourself at risk to impregnate someone or to become pregnant. You're also putting yourself at risk to contract a sexually transmitted disease (STD). Condoms reduce the odds of pregnancy and STDs. Still, condoms are not a 100% guarantee against contracting an STD, nor are they the most effective means of birth control. If you can't talk with your parents about sex or contraceptives, find another mature adult whom you trust, and talk with them. It's better to talk with someone who's mature and who can give you accurate information about sex, birth control and STDs rather than with a friend who doesn't know any more than you do!

I get accurate information about sex from mature, informed adults who care about me.

October 4

There were two events in my life that were extremely important. The first was graduating from college. The second was accomplishing the goal of getting into graduate school even though I am dyslexic.
—Ennis William Cosby

If you're trying as hard as you can to get good grades but have problems concentrating when your teacher is teaching, you may have a learning disorder. If you have dyslexia like Ennis, the letters in words seem to jump around the page when you try to read. You also have trouble taking in information, and you feel confused. If you suffer from a learning disability you may think you're stupid or slow. You're not! Most kids with learning disorders have average or above average intelligence. Because parents and teachers know you're not stupid, they may think you're lazy or you don't care about school. But you do care! *There is help for you if you have a learning disability.* Ennis got help with his disability and he achieved so much in spite of it. He earned both a bachelor's and a master's degree, and he helped other kids deal with their dyslexia. And if Ennis did it, you can too!

I do well in school despite my learning disability.

October 5

No matter if you're handicapped, HIV-positive, whatever it is—just keep living!
—Earvin "Magic" Johnson

Unlike dyslexia and other learning disabilities people can't see, if you have a physical disability, people probably can see your disability. But your physical disability doesn't make you any less valuable than anybody else. Your friends may not understand that if you're limited or handicapped in one area of your life, you more than make up for it in other areas. You're really not disabled, just differently abled. Like "Magic" says, if you're handicapped or battling leukemia, cancer, HIV or any other life-threatening disease, *just keep living!* If you know someone who has a terminal illness, stay up for them. I know it's tough, but it helps them if you're positive about their disease. My brother, Matthew Willis died of acute lymphatic leukemia at age 28. But, just like "Magic," Matthew never let his disease stop him from living while he still had breath! He wrote the entry on March 7, his birthday, before he died.

I am living my life to the fullest!

October 6

I grew up learning that women were bitches and whores and sex objects. Those notions eventually contributed to a lot of my destructive behavior toward myself and toward black women.
—Nathan McCall

When you grow up watching your mothers or your sisters or your aunts being treated like dogs, you run the risk of believing that women should be treated like dogs. Women are not bitches! Women are not whores! Women are not sex objects! Women and girls may get on your nerves, make you cry, make you laugh, run out on you, cheat on you, be there for you, be your best friend, help you when you most need help, excite you, tease you, care about you, manipulate you, talk to you, ignore you, befriend you or love you. Women or girls may do all these things and then some. No matter what women or girls do or don't do, they are not bitches, whores or sex objects. Women and girls are mothers and grandmothers and aunts and sisters and friends and girlfriends who are human just like you.

I respect the ladies.

October 7

He may say that he loves you. Wait and see what he does for you!

—Senegalese Proverb

There are ways to show someone you love them and there are things you do which disprove your love for someone. When you love someone, you trust them. When you love someone, you don't continually judge them—you learn to accept them as they are. When you love someone, you tell them how much you love them and you mean it. When you love someone, you want good things to happen to them, and you're not threatened by their success. When you love someone, you give them a shoulder to lean on when they're down, but you never make it comfortable for them to stay down. When you love someone, you give the best of yourself to them because you feel they deserve the best you have to give. Love is the most precious thing you can give to someone, and it's the gift people want more than anything else in the world.

I know the true meaning of love.

October 8

We must teach our children to trust their hopes and not their fears.

—Dr. Eleta Greene

Fear is learned. And fear can have a healthy place in our lives. Too often, though, we live with unhealthy fears—fears that paralyze us and keep us from living up to our potential. Faith overcomes fear. Repeating your affirmations can help you eliminate your fears. Try this: Just before you fall asleep at night and when you first wake up in the morning, program your mind with only positive thoughts and affirmations. Visualize in your mind the positive outcomes you want to happen during the day. Remember, what your mind can see, it can make real, whether good or bad. Everyone has fears and negative thoughts, but you've got to learn not to concentrate on your fears and negative thoughts. Faith that your higher power is protecting you and helping you along your way lets you know you have nothing to fear!

As I look out into the world, I know I have nothing to fear.

October 9

I mean, that was the first Christmas that I actually woke up and saw her open up her presents. It was like, man this is the best time I ever had in my life.
>
> —William Gates, star of *Hoop Dreams*

If you're a teenage father and you're not involved in your child's life, you're missing out on so much. Sure babies cry, their diapers need changing and they demand a lot from you. But babies are also very giving. Your daughter is waiting for you to give her love, so she can give it right back to you. Your son is waiting for you to give him a smile and a laugh so he can smile back at cha' and show off his pint-size laugh. Your child is waiting for you to show him who he's supposed to be! And as you show her, she has so much to show you. She has a song she learned in preschool to sing to you. Your son has artwork for you to hang on your refrigerator door. He also has a boo-boo to show you. You see, if you've fathered a child and you're not involved in his or her life, you're missing out on so much!

When I give my child love, he gives it right back to me!

October 10

I tell the kids from struggle comes strength. And if everything's easy, then how do you know how to survive when inevitably, there comes a time when things aren't so happy-go-lucky.
—Jada Pinkett Smith

Do you have it rough? Even at your young age have you already had a rough life? Are you jealous of kids whom you think have had it easy? Kids who come from well off families, kids who are lighter skinned than you or kids whom you think are smarter or more athletic than you? Just because someone's parents' have more money than yours or their skin is lighter than yours doesn't automatically mean they have it any easier than you. If you're jealous of kids who don't seem to have any problems, talk to them in 15 years. Why? Because like Jada says, from struggle comes strength. The rough times you're going through now will make you stronger—if you get through them and learn from them. And in 15 years, when you're a mature adult, other adults who haven't learned how to cope when things are rough might just be jealous of you!

I grow stronger when I get through the difficult times in my life.

October 11

I didn't have a messed up childhood. I had a beautiful childhood. I didn't have a father, but I had love. My mother was always there making sure things were great for me, and I had my grandmother who did the same.

— Sean "Puffy" Combs

Some of you reading this are having wonderful childhoods just life Puffy. Others of you aren't. Hey! Everybody's life is different. What we can all understand is *it's not what happens to us when we're young that determines how we'll end up in life, it's how we respond and react to what happens.* No matter what circumstances you find yourself in, always remember what you're made of. You're made of love! Love lives inside you! You are love! No matter what's going on outside you, *remember your love.* Remember that you're the one who's really in control of your life, even though it may not seem that way. And remember that your higher power is always there for you even if your mother, your father or whoever isn't!

The love I have inside keeps me safe and secure.

October 12

I don't think you should allow yourself to become jaded. There's a choice: Just because you see ugliness doesn't mean you have to become it, or even necessarily believe in it too wholeheartedly.
—Jewel

Kidnappings. Murder. War. Drugs. Gang violence. Government corruption. Child molestation. Rape. Terrorist bombs! There is a lot of ugliness in our world today. But there is also so much beauty. There are good things happening in the world, it's just that you hear more about the bad things. For example, there are teachers committed to helping their students be the best they can be. Okay, so there are some bad teachers out there, but there are still *many good teachers*. If things are bad for you, you tend to think everything is all messed up! And if things are good for you, you tend to be more optimistic about the world. What we can all try to do is heed Jewel's advice. Believe in the good things and don't let the ugliness get you down.

In spite of everything, I am optimistic about our world.

October 13

Your own soul is nourished when you are kind; it is destroyed when you are cruel.
—Proverbs 11:17

When you're mean to other people, you hurt them and abuse them, but you also hurt and abuse yourself. When you're kind to other people, your acts of kindness lift them up and make them feel better, but they also make you feel better and bring good things into your life. How does this work? Simple—what you do to others will be done to you. So if you want others to be kind to you, try being kind to others. If you want respect from others, then respect others. If you don't want people to steal things from you, then don't you steal things from them. If you don't want people always talking about you behind your back and doggin' you out, then you stop doggin' out so many people. Of course, if you'd rather have people disrespecting you, doggin' you out and being mean to you...

I treat others the way I want them to treat me.

October 14

I was always so afraid to be accepted for who I am.
It took me a while to realize that being different is
okay.

—Greg Louganis

Wouldn't it be wonderful to feel as though everyone
accepted you for who you are? Wonderful to feel
totally loved, respected and approved of? If you do
feel loved, respected and approved of, you know
that's the greatest feeling there is! It feels great when
you feel accepted even if you are different from other
kids. But even though it's perfectly normal for you to
want to be accepted, don't spend all your precious
energy trying to make people like you or accept you
because not everyone will. When you really believe
you're special and important, you'll spend a lot less
time trying to be accepted by everybody and a lot
more time just being you. Don't hate yourself because
you're different from other kids. And don't think
there's something wrong with you if you're gay. Just
remember, it's okay to be different.

*I love me for who I am, and I realize it's okay to be
different.*

October 15

I value her because I appreciate her truthfulness. She knows how to keep it real. And she really cracks me up.

—One cool boyfriend

Teenage boys responses when asked "If girls acted the way you wanted them to, how would they act?" Girls in general they'll be like 'ooh, he's ugly' and they don't try to get to know you, they just look at the outside. • Some girls don't say what they want. They beat around the bush sometimes. Like if I ask a question and I don't get any feedback, how am I going to know how to do this and how to do that and how to help out the relationship? • They wouldn't act crazy. They wouldn't be trying to think they too good for people. Some of them think they too good for people. • If I'm going out of my way speaking to them and they want to try to act like they Miss America and too good to speak, I don't have time for that. It's their attitude that makes them ugly. • They would be themselves instead of someone they're not. • Nicer, more polite. Nowadays, they don't talk to you in the right way.

I treat boys with respect, and I'm honest and open with them.

October 16

I love him because he's got such a gentle spirit. And he's gentle and loving with everybody not just me.
—An equally cool girlfriend

Teenage girls responses when asked, "If boys acted the way you wanted them to, how would they act?" They would treat you with respect. They'd be sensitive to your feelings—some guys just don't have feelings at all. • They would be honest and stop lying about stuff. • The guys I deal with don't know how to say sorry, and they don't know how to admit when they're wrong, and I hate that. • Nowadays they're man enough to call you and ask you to be their girl, but when they're with their boys or other people, they say 'that's not my girl, I don't mess with her like that, we're just friends.' But when you're alone it's about 'you know you're my one and only, you're the only one for me' and so on etcetera. But if you're man enough to ask a girl to be with you, then you're man enough to keep that relationship outside around other people, and if not, you shouldn't try to step in the first place.

I treat girls with respect, and I'm honest and open with them.

October 17

It's hard to look a certain way and move through this world with self-confidence.
—Fatima Faloye

White. Pale. Light, bright and damned near white. High yellow. Light-skinned. Butterscotch. Red-boned. Honey brown. Milk Chocolate. Black. Charcoal. Midnight. Ink Spot. Blue-eyed. Long and Blond. Brown-eyed. Short and Nappy. Kinky. Big-boned. Fat. A whale. A blimp. Petite. Little. Skinny. A toothpick. Big lips. Big hips. No butt. Bubble-eyed. Four-eyed. Ugly. Pretty. Fine. A dog face. Scary! Yes, it is hard to look a certain way and move through this world with self-confidence. It's hard, but it's not impossible. It's not impossible when you refuse to let the media convince you that the only beautiful people are blond-haired, blue-eyed, thin or "ideal weight" people who could pose for a magazine cover!

My body and my looks don't have to be "perfect" for me to be okay.

October 18

I believe that one positive thought creates millions of positive vibrations.
—Carlos Santana

I am happy because people love me. When I feel happy, I want to smile at everybody I see. I have peace inside because I know things are going to work out for me. When I feel at peace, I don't even think about anything negative. When my friends and I get together, I feel good because I know they care about me and will be there for me. I'm fortunate to have such good friends. Even though everything in my life right now is not exactly the way I want it, I know my life will be successful. Knowing that I'm going to make it keeps me going! Go ahead, take out a piece of paper and a pen and write down your own positive thoughts. Write down 10 things you're thankful for. And don't be surprised at how good you feel when you take some time to think about everything that's good in your life!

I give myself permission to be positive.

October 19

Every time I don't listen to my inner voice, I'm
headed down the wrong road. Every time I do listen
to it, I always benefit.
—Des'ree

Everybody has an inner voice that will keep us on the
right path and help keep us safe. That inner voice is
your spirit. That inner voice is your higher self or
your higher power. The only way, though, to
recognize your inner voice is to stay connected with
your spirit. When you're connected, you'll know
when something is right for you or not right for you
because your spirit will tell you. Your spirit tells you,
not with words, necessarily, but through feeling and
intuition. This communication between you and your
spirit is what makes you a more spiritual being.
Being spiritual means striving to feel God, or in
others words—*love*—in everything and in everyone.
As you become more spiritual, you'll see that more
things begin to work out for you. Like Des'ree says,
when you listen to your inner voice, you always
benefit.

*I trust my higher power, and I listen to my inner
voice.*

October 20

I try to be as present in my life as I can be, and whatever can get me to that place I think of as being spiritual practices.

—Susan Sarandon

What does Susan mean when she says she tries to be as "present" in her life as she can? She means she tries not to worry about tomorrow. Too many of us worry too much! When we learn to live in the present, we can stop all this worrying. One way to do this is to be thankful for everything you've got going for you now. When you take time out to look at the good in your life today, you're not as stressed about tomorrow. And when you begin to be happy and content with what you have, even if what you have isn't much, then you're ready to accept more. And more will come to you. Your higher power will provide it for you! When you understand that what you need will come to you in the right time, there's really no need to worry!

I am thankful for the good things in my life right now!

October 21

If you offend, ask for a pardon; if offended, forgive.
—Ethiopian Proverb

The reason it's so important for you to forgive others when they mess up, make a mistake or do you wrong is because one day, you're going to mess up, make a mistake or do somebody wrong. The reason it works this way is because nobody is perfect. You need to forgive so that you can be forgiven. The people who are the least forgiving of others are almost always the ones who demand that others forgive them when they mess up. If you're having a hard time forgiving people, it's because you haven't forgiven yourself. Nobody is perfect! If you know people who want you to act perfectly or do things perfectly, they're the ones with the problem, not you. It's impossible to lead a perfect life. And forgiveness makes it okay for you and me and everybody else to mess up, to be human.

I forgive myself and others, and others forgive me.

October 22

I know how scary it is to be 18 and legally on your own but with nowhere to go.
—Victoria Rowell

At age two-and-a-half, Victoria and her two sisters went to live with a foster family. And like she says, if you're in foster care and about to turn 18 *or* graduate from high school, you're probably scared. Even though you're sick of being told what to do by the county and ready to get your driver's license, you still don't want to be left completely on your own. You're probably wondering where you'll live, how you'll support yourself, and who you'll depend on for emotional support now that your caseworker, your counselors and your foster parents won't always be there for you? Many states have foster care transitional or independent living programs for 16-, 17- and 18-year-olds. Some programs even run until you turn 21. Find out what's available in your state.

Graduating from high school and becoming a young adult may be scary, but there are people who can help me.

October 23

My mom always said 'What goes around comes around.'"

—Jesse Jackson Jr.

If your mom or dad or grandmother or grandfather has always told you what goes around comes around, they were telling the truth. When you look at how your life is going now and where your life is headed you can probably see that what goes around comes around. If you examine your life and find good, peace and happiness in it, that's because you've been good, you haven't made war on others and you haven't been the cause of unhappiness for others. If you examine your life and you're not happy with what you find, tell yourself two things: "I can change my life," and "What goes around comes around." You determine what kind of life you'll have by the thoughts you think, the words you speak and the actions you take. Knowing that, you'd be wise to think good thoughts, affirm positive situations for yourself and treat others the way you want to be treated!

I think, speak and act in ways that will bring me peace, happiness and a good life.

October 24

Women don't have to put up with physical abuse in their own household. We can do without that.
—Dionne Farris

If your boyfriend has ever pushed you, cursed at you or is extremely jealous and overprotective of you, then he has abused you. Most abusive relationships begin with verbal and emotional abuse. The next thing you know, you've been beaten up. If you think it's great to have a boyfriend who's extremely jealous, and if you think his jealousy means he loves you, you're mistaking jealousy for love. Sometimes, when your boyfriend is abusive, you think it's your fault. You think you deserve the abuse as punishment for something you did wrong. Nobody is perfect, and we all mess up sometimes, but you don't deserve to be hit or punished by your boyfriend for anything. You have the right to express your opinions. You have the right to change your mind. You deserve to be treated right. And you should not be hit or slapped or cursed at or humiliated or controlled by your boyfriend!

I have the right to be treated right.

October 25

We had to learn to be men.
—Nathan Morris of Boyz II Men

Unfortunately, some boys learn that to be real men, they have to control women. Boys who grow up in homes where their fathers curse, slap or hit their mothers may learn it's okay to treat women this way. It's not okay. It's not masculine and it doesn't make you more of man to hit and abuse girls. It also doesn't make you more of a man to allow your girl to abuse you, either physically or emotionally. Men and boys who are with women and girls who fight them often feel embarrassed. If you're in a relationship and you're being abused by your girlfriend either emotionally or physically, you need help. If you're in a relationship and you're abusing your girlfriend, you need help. You can get help by calling the National Domestic Violence Hotline at 800-799-SAFE.

I am learning how to have healthy relationships.

October 26

We argue sometimes, but we don't hold any grudges.
—Maxee of Brownstone

Friends argue, mothers and fathers argue, coworkers argue, brothers and sisters argue, business partners argue. Arguing and disagreeing is a part of life because everybody has an opinion. Sometimes, you think someone else's opinions are wack. So what! They sometimes think the same thing about your opinions. In life, you've got to accept that people are different and therefore, will have different opinions and ideas. But different opinions and ideas aren't always wrong—sometimes they're just different. When you begin to understand that not everybody sees things the way you see them, you'll stop getting so angry at everybody. Everybody has a right to express who they are. When you disagree with friends, family or strangers, that's okay. What's not okay is to hold grudges and to stay mad because they don't see things the way you do.

I don't have to agree with everybody and everybody doesn't have to agree with me.

October 27

Lord when I've done the best that I can/ and my best
is not good enough/ Lord help me to understand/ that
being a good parent is very tough.
—a poem by Mamie Marie Willis

Being a good parent *is* very tough. It becomes
tougher when kids reach puberty and become
teenagers. If your relationship with your parents
changed from good to bad or from bad to worse when
you became a teenager, don't worry. That happens in
many families. Why? Teenagers are naturally
rebellious because you're at the stage where you're
trying to assert your independence. You often want
more freedom and independence than parents want to
give. Becoming independent is a natural part of
growing up. But even though it seems like your mom
became the Wicked Witch of the West when you
became a teenager, she didn't! Your mom, your dad,
your foster parents, your grandparents, whoever is
raising you has the hardest job on earth. They love
you and are doing the best they can. Sometimes their
best is real good, you just don't realize it.

*My parents are doing the best they know how, and I
appreciate them.*

October 28

I didn't have much of a family. So that lack of family has me hungering for my own.
—Kirk Franklin

Oftentimes, kids who run away from home don't feel as though they have much of a family. If you've run away, you know how it feels to be on the streets, hungry and feeling all alone with seemingly nowhere to go. If you're in a messed-up home situation and you've thought about running away, or if you know someone who's considering running way, here's some information for you The Covenant House operates a nationwide, toll-free hotline for teenagers who need help. It's called the 9-Line and the number is 800-999-9999. Counselors at the 9-Line have a listing of approximately 26,000 social service agencies in all 50 states—agencies you may not be aware of. If you're thinking about running away, or if you're having other problems, call the 9-Line and they'll connect you with people nearby who can probably help you get through your difficult times.

There is help for me!

October 29

It's up to me to get my confidence back.
—Michelle Kwan

Michelle Kwan was the world figure skating champ in 1996. A year later, she had some disappointing performances and she lost her confidence. You can lose confidence in yourself, and you can lose confidence in other people. Sometimes, those people are adults. When adults don't do the right things, it's natural for you to lose confidence in them. It's natural not to trust people who've abused you. But if you go through life thinking you can't trust anybody, you'll probably keep some bad people from hurting you, but you'll also keep some good people from helping you. You may not believe this, but everybody is not out to get you. If an adult has abused you or violated your trust, talk to a licensed therapist about the abuse so you can get your trust and your confidence back.

I know there are good people out there who want to help me be the best I can be!

October 30

People who hurt other people have usually been hurt so badly themselves that all they know how to do is hurt back.
—Terry McMillan

Everybody has scars from the past. But some people who've suffered painful pasts, don't strike out at others. Instead, they inflict pain on themselves. Estimates are that nearly two million people hurt themselves by cutting, biting or burning themselves. People who injure themselves do so because they need to express the emotional pain they feel, but don't know how to in healthy ways. Many kids who injure themselves have parents who are high achievers but who have trouble communicating their feelings. Kids who injure themselves are often intelligent, sensitive kids with low self-esteem. But cutting or burning yourself when you're upset or feeling overwhelmed by your emotional pain can only give you temporary relief. It's just like using alcohol or drugs to deal with pain. It doesn't work, and it can mess you up bad.

I am learning how to express my pain in healthy ways.

October 31

We can overcome or succumb.
—Morgan Freeman

Hey you! Don't give up! I know it's hard sometimes.
I know you get depressed. I know things don't always
work out for you. Sometimes, it seems as though
nothing goes your way. But don't give up and give
in. You can make it! You've done it before. Things
have been rough for you before and you didn't give
up. You stuck in there and you overcame. You
survived. You may have forgotten just how strong
you are. Remind yourself now. You come from a
long line of strong people. People who overcame all
kinds of hardships. People who have been
discriminated against and treated unfairly—and
people who didn't give up! You're just like them.
You can overcome! You don't have to succumb.
When you face up to your struggles and overcome
them, you become a stronger person. Life has many
lessons it wants you to learn. And learning is
sometimes a painful process. *But, it's all good!* You
can do it. You can overcome!

I never give up!

November 1

God give us grace to accept with serenity the things that cannot be changed, courage to change the things which should be changed, and the wisdom to distinguish the one from the other.

—Reinhold Niebuhr, The Serenity
Prayer

How do you react when something bad happens to you? There are two choices you can make when bad things happen. You can choose to accept or not to accept what has happened. When something bad happens and you don't or won't accept it, you begin fighting it. But it's a losing fight because once something has happened, you can't make it unhappen. When you accept the bad things that happen in life, you put yourself in a much better position to get over them. Some of the bad things going on today are out of your control. Don't stress things you can't control or change. Some of the bad things in your life, however, are there because of things you did or didn't do. You don't have to like those things, but you do have to accept them. Accept that you've made some mistakes, learn from your mistakes and move on.

I am smart enough to know what I can and cannot change, and I change the things I can.

November 2

If you live your whole life guided by external forces,
you're dead before you even die.
—Quincy Jones

What does Quincy mean by external forces? He
means those things you can't change or control. Like
when someone tells you you're no good or you're
ugly or stupid. Those words come from other people's
mouths, and yes, those words hurt! But even though
being dissed and talked about hurts, you don't have to
let it control you. When someone tells you you're no
good, tell yourself just how good you are. When
anyone—a teacher, a friend or a parent—criticizes
you, understand that criticism, no matter how bad it
feels, never makes you a bad person. If the person
criticizing you is trying to help you, accept their
criticism and learn from it. But if they're trying to tear
you down and make you out to be some kind of awful
person, remind yourself just how good you are, and
ignore them!

I believe in myself! I am a good person!

November 3

Look around you. We all have a responsibility to each other as people.
—Bryce Wilson of Groove Theory

Have you noticed that when a few people mess up , it affects everybody? The reason the downstairs bathroom in the public library is locked at six o'clock every night and everybody has to use the children's bathroom upstairs is because a few teenagers kept vandalizing the downstairs bathroom. The reason your school installed metal detectors is because some students decided to act in ways that put all students' lives in peril. It's sometimes hard for teenagers to understand you're part of something larger than just yourselves, your friends, and your family. As you get older you'll better understand the notion that what you do affects yourself and everyone else alive! You'll understand that when you steal clothes from stores, the stores raise the prices to make up for the millions of dollars in theft they incur each year, and your thievery causes everybody to pay more for their clothes!

I am a responsible citizen of the world.

November 4

When I signed the deal, I was 19 and arrogant. You couldn't tell me anything—couldn't tell me how to sing or what to write. Man, I knew it all. I had a lot of growing up to do—as a person and as an artist.
—Brian McKnight

Sometimes, when you're 11, you think you know it all. Sometimes, when you turn 13 or 16, you suddenly think you know it all. And most people probably thought they knew it all by the time they were 19, just like Brian. Word! You may be the top high school sprinter in the nation. You may have a 4.2 grade point average. You may be making mad money as a teenager, either legally or illegally. You may have been right about something everyone else swore you were wrong about. So! You still don't know it all. Not at age 11, 13, 16, 19, 25, 40, 60, 80 or 100. No one knows all there is to know.

I am constantly learning and growing and changing for the better.

November 5

When I wake up in the morning and I'm too tired to brush my teeth, AIDS says, 'I got you.'
—Rae Lewis-Thornton

Don't let AIDS get you! AIDS is caused by the HIV virus. And yes, you can have HIV and not look sick or feel sick or nothing. Word! HIV can hang around for as long as 10 years before becoming AIDS. That means that kids in their early 20s who have AIDS could have become infected with HIV when they were as young as 10! Sexually active girls are at even greater risks than sexually active boys of becoming infected with HIV. Why? Because a girl's vaginal lining can break easily during sex and give HIV an easy way to get into her system. If you already have a venereal disease, it's also easier for HIV to penetrate. But you don't have to contract HIV or any sexually transmitted disease. Talk with a mature, informed adult or call the Centers for Disease Control STD hotline at 800-227-8922 from 8:00 a.m. to 11:00 p.m. EST to learn more about venereal diseases.

I know the real deal on sexually transmitted diseases and how I can keep from getting them.

November 6

We will not bow down to racism! We will not bow down to injustice! We will not bow down to exploitation! I'm gon stand! I'm gon stand!
> —Sung *by Sweet Honey in the Rock,* composed by Bernice Johnson Reagon

As you've read repeatedly in this book, racism has power over you only if you let it. The way to overcome racism is to never believe you're inferior even though some ignorant, racist people might. Sometimes, though, that's not enough. There are times when you must stand up to racism and fight it. That's what activism is about! Sometimes, you have to do what your ancestors did when their lands were being invaded, when they were being enslaved, and when they couldn't vote. You have to fight back! You have to organize, protest, march, sign petitions, stage sit-ins and demand that racist and unfair practices cease and desist! Never bow down to racism. Never bow down to injustice. Never bow down to exploitation. Take action! Take a stand!

I take a stand against racism!

November 7

Speak out against racism and sexism.
—Kweisi Mfume

Sexism, like racism, is a fact of life in the world we live in. Some of you go to schools where the girls play just as hard to win their basketball games as the boys, but don't get the same recognition as the boys. Some of you live in homes where the girls have to clean, cook and help out at home and the boys aren't required to do anything. In some homes, girls have one curfew and the boys have a different, more lenient one. Some of you sit in classes where teachers call on boys for answers and interact more often with the boys than with the girls. But girls are just as intelligent as boys. And boys are just as capable of helping out at home as girls. Neither racist nor sexist attitudes will change overnight, but if you, *boys and girls alike,* don't start speaking out against these harmful discriminatory attitudes, they'll never change.

I take a stand against sexist ideas and attitudes!

November 8

I always believe there is a possibility for good. I am the eternal optimist.
—Rep. Maxine Waters

Do you know people who are always getting into trouble? If you had to predict their future, you'd probably predict a bad one, right? Not if you're an optimist. You see, optimists, and people who've taught themselves to look for the good in others, know that people are forever changing. The kid who's always getting into trouble today could be the adult who ends up helping others stay out of trouble tomorrow. The nerd or the class clown today could be the serious businessman or the accomplished movie star tomorrow. As you mature and grow, you'll learn that people aren't all good or all bad or all anything. You'll also see that people can and do change. Like Maxine says, there's always a possibility for good. And even the meanest acting lowlife has some good in him or her!

I am learning to see the good in others.

November 9

Everyone dreams of being something or someone. The deal is for you to pick the dream suitable for you and take the right road to get where you want to go.

—Wanya Morris of Boyz II Men

How many ways can you tell someone it's up to them to make their life the way they want it to be? "It ain't nothing to it but to do it." "Just do it." Well, it's not always easy to just do it. And what about when you fail? Sometimes when you fail, you feel embarrassed, and you think, "I should have never wasted my time trying that." Well, everybody fails sometimes, and you'll do yourself a big favor if you remember that failing doesn't mean the end. Failing doesn't mean you should stop trying. It means you should try something different! Wanya says pick the dream suitable to you then take the right road to get where you want to go. Sometimes, though, you have to go down the wrong road before you figure out it's not the right road. That's okay. If you don't let failure stop you, you'll achieve what you set out to achieve.

It may take a while, but nothing will stop me from reaching my goals.

November 10

The problem isn't the value the kids put on the sneakers, it's the lack of value some of them put on human life.

—Grant Hill

Let's talk about life! In life, the need to fit in and have the coolest sneakers, clothes or car is one of the strongest needs you have. What have you done recently to try to fit in with the crowd? Did your parents find out about it? If so, how did they react? Now let's talk about value. What does it even mean to value a human life? When you value someone, you care about that person and you show them you care by taking care of them. Instead of abusing them or trying to waste them or get rid of them, you protect them. What is your life is worth? What is your best friend's life worth. How about your worst enemy if you have one? The worth of someone's life can never be measured in dollars or things. There is no amount of money, clothes, cars or sneakers that can ever replace a life.

I value and respect life.

November 11

My mother said that when people call you disadvantaged and underprivileged, they're talking about your income. And you can't let your income determine your outcome.

—Rep. Cleo Fields

How much of a disadvantage are you really at when you have parents who love you and work hard to feed and clothe you? How underprivileged can you really be when you're being reared by a single father or a single mother who does everything he or she can to see that you're happy and healthy and taken care of? Like legislator Cleo Fields says, you can't let your parents' income determine whether you succeed in life. If your parents are working class or poor, don't let the amount of money they make or don't make become an excuse for you not being successful. If you have a loving and supportive family, and if you believe in you, you have everything you need to be successful. It's your attitude, not how much or how little money you have, that determines your outcome.

I am going to make it in life, no matter what!

November 12

I was one of those kids who looked in magazines and saw nice cars and nice houses and thought, Wow, one day I'd like things like that.
—Seal

There's nothing wrong with wanting nice cars, houses or money. But as you've been told by people with lots of money, money does not bring happiness. Sinbad told you that on January 29. Money can never bring nor buy inner peace as Babyface said on March 1. And money cannot buy you true security. Mike Tyson said that on August 16. Seal dreamed of having nice things as a kid, and guess what? He survived being homeless from the time he was 15, and he later became a singing star, and he got the nice things he'd dreamed about. Affirm in your mind what kind of life you want for yourself, believe you *deserve* the kind of life you say you want, then do everything necessary to make your dream come true. But don't think for one second that having lots of money is going to bring you happiness, peace of mind or security.

Life is ready to give me everything that is good.

November 13

I've acquired inner peace and serenity.
— Q-Tip of A Tribe Called Quest

If money doesn't bring about happiness, security or inner peace, what does? Different people will answer that differently. I've gained happiness, security and inner peace by trusting my higher power and by understanding the spiritual laws that govern the universe. What spiritual laws? The law of giving and receiving that says whatever you give away, you get back. Many people think when they give something away they've lost it. Not true! Whether it's your money, your love, your time, your possessions, your anger, your hatred—whatever you give away, you get back! The law of abundance says you'll get those things in life you're willing to accept and believe you can have—no more and no less. Because I believe my higher power wants me to have everything that's good, I know that, even when it seems as if things aren't going to work out for the best, they will! Now that's inner peace.

I am happy, secure and filled with inner peace and serenity.

November 14

Don't trap yourself in just one line of believing and one line of thinking. If you start opening your mind up, you'll start seeing it's a real big world out here, and there's a lot of great thinkers you can take a little piece from and put your own puzzle together.
—Kid Sensation

In life, you have to figure out how to put the pieces of your life's puzzle together. Your beliefs will determine how you assemble your puzzle. Everyone has a belief system even if you're not aware of what yours is. Most people get their beliefs and their belief systems from what their parents teach them about life, about right and wrong and about God. As you grow and mature and change, your belief system will probably grow and mature and change, if you keep an open mind! When you keep an open mind, you understand that what's right for you may not be right for someone else and vice versa. When you keep an open mind, you allow yourself and others room to grow and change and be exposed to new thoughts and ideas.

New thoughts and ideas are coming to me, and I keep an open mind.

November 15

I became smart because everybody expected me to
be. I became intelligent.
—John Singleton

It's great when your family, friends and teachers
expect you to achieve what you're capable of
achieving. But if you don't have teachers who
encourage you, friends who've told you how talented
you are, or parents who expect the best from you,
you're just going to have to begin expecting the best
from yourself! You're going to have to motivate
yourself. When you're self motivated, and when you
expect great things from yourself, you'll achieve great
things. You are intelligent, however, if you don't
know it, you won't show it. But, if you expect to get
good grades, and if you expect to do well in school,
you'll begin to do well in school. Once you start
achieving success, those who didn't expect great
things from you will!

*I expect great things from myself even if no one else
does!*

November 16

There were a lot of drugs and violence around. I pretty much stayed out of it, although some of my best friends from home are in jail—and won't be out for a while.

—Deion Sanders

Do you know people who are caught up in drugs or violence? Do you know people who are locked up? Just because your friends are caught up in drugs or violence or acting without considering the consequences of their actions doesn't mean you have to be. There are other choices you can make. As a teenager you'll have to make many choices and decisions. Sometimes, your friends won't like the decisions you make. They may get angry with you. They may make fun of you—call you a punk. But isn't it better to be called a punk than to be locked up? Isn't it better to face the consequences that come with not giving in to your friends than it is to go along with them and do something that will cause you to be in jail for a long time?

I make choices that keep me happy, healthy and out of trouble.

November 17

Arresting people just isn't the answer. Education is the answer....The message I want to give to kids and their parents is that the kids are our future.
—Officer J.H. Carpenter

Throughout the country, there are police officers who try to help you before you do something that can get you locked up. Officers like J.H. Carpenter in Bethlehem, Pennsylvania. who would rather teach you than beat you. Officers like James "Eddie Murphy" Martin, Eric "21" Davis and Randy "Faheem" Holcomb, who, in 1992, began performing rap songs in schools throughout the country. The Slick Boys, as the undercover cops are known, visit schools on their days off and rap about staying in school and away from drugs, gangs and crime. Remember, there are good cops out there just like there are cops out there who don't give a damn about you. Ultimately, though, it's up to you to decide whether you'll stay out of trouble and out of jail or in trouble and in the system.

I am the future, and I am helping to make the future of the world something good!

November 18

You have to raise children from birth to age 12 because after that, you can't raise them anymore; you can only give them advice and guidance if you have a good relationship.

—Terry Lewis

Childrearing can be rewarding! Here are a few helpful hints for teenage parents. Try not to yell at your kid because it hurts his self-esteem. When he messes up, discipline him, and make him understand that what he did was bad, but that he's still a great kid! That way, his self-esteem stays cool and he learns right from wrong. And when you talk to him, stoop down to his level and make eye contact with him because he'll better understand what you're trying to tell him. It also helps to give kids choices so they learn to have confidence and a sense of control. At lunchtime when he's outside playing, ask him, "Do you want to eat outside or in the kitchen?" He'll probably be more willing to stop playing and *come in* and eat than if you yell, "You gotta stop playing and come eat now!"

I am helping my child develop a positive self-esteem.

November 19

My own need for parenting exceeded my ability to be one.

—Richard Pryor

There are grown men who have a hard time being good parents because even though their age says they're adults, emotionally, they're still little kids! If you're a teenage father you're probably not emotionally prepared to be a parent either. So now what? You could abandon your child, and let the kid grow up without ever knowing his or her father. You could just pay child support and never visit, talk to or hang with your child. Or you could be responsible and become involved in your child's life. If you take on the responsibility of raising your kid, understand that you're deciding to become a man! Men take care of their kids. Boys make babies and forget about them. If you choose to be a man and be responsible, go to a father who's doing a good job raising his children and ask for his advice on being a good dad.

I am a man who takes care of his kids.

November 20

You just got to keep on doing what you're doing and work it out.

—LL Cool J.

Some things take time. And sometimes, it's so hard to wait. Why? Because you're impatient. Because you want it now—wanted it yesterday! Well, if you're lacking patience, now is a good time to develop some. How? Learn to appreciate everything you have right now. Take time out to look at the good in your life today. When you can be happy with what you have, even if what you have isn't much, you're ready to accept more. And more will come to you. It will find you! Nobody's life is exactly the way he or she wants it to be all the time. But people who are the most happy and the most content have learned not to become angry or resentful about what's not right lives or about what's missing in their lives. It's only when we allow whatever circumstances we face to make us better, not bitter, that we get the good life has to offer.

I am patiently working things out for me.

November 21

Think yourself a queen and you are a queen. Think that you, a single mother without a job, can be a success and success will follow.
—Susan L. Taylor

If you're a single teenage mother who's decided not to stay in school, you probably think you have a good reason for dropping out. Maybe you never liked school anyway. Maybe there would be no one else to care for your baby if you were to continue with school. If you've quit school, it's not too late to return. Why go back? Because you need your education if you and your baby are going to make it in life. But like Susan says, the only way to get a good job and become successful or stay in school and do well is to believe you can. Remember, if you think you're a queen, you'll start acting like a queen, and soon, everybody will be calling you "Ms. Queen!" You can finish school. It's not impossible. Many girls have babies, stay in school and later march across that stage with their diploma in hand while their baby cheers and claps for Mommy. You can too!

I am a successful teenage mother making choices that will help me and my child.

November 22

> I was never disappointed for myself, only that I had let down the people of Japan. I have no regrets because I know I did my best—all I could do.
> —Midori Ito

Olympic figure skater, Midori Ito, didn't win the gold medal in the 1992 Olympics as was expected of her by her entire country. She did, however, win the silver medal, *and she did her best.* Sometimes, you don't live up to your own or others' expectations, and, unlike Midori, you do have regrets. Word! There is nothing wrong with finishing second or third. When you don't finish first, you may feel like a failure. You're not! There's a reason why you fail. There's a reason why you come in second instead of first. Failing teaches you that you have more to learn. And your failures bring you that much closer to your successes—unless you quit trying. It's okay to stop trying if you decide you'd rather do something else. But don't give up because you're discouraged or frustrated. Try again, but try a different way! Always do your best and you'll never have anything to regret.

I'm always a winner because I always do my best.

November 23

I was living on the Northside, and some guys from the Southside came over. Me and my friend were just sitting in the truck, and I saw them circle around us about five or six times.

—Anfernee Hardaway "Penny"

After the guys in the car circled around Penny and his friend several times, they pulled up and asked for directions. Four men then jumped out, pointed their guns and told Penny and his friend to hit the ground. The guys took money, shoes, jewelry and began to drive away. When they'd driven about 100 feet, they stopped their car and fired shots at Penny and his friend. A bullet hit Penny in the foot. Penny was a freshman at Memphis State when the shooting occurred in 1991. *He became a millionaire NBA superstar.* You may be minding your business and, suddenly find yourself in a bad situation just like Penny. If that happens, don't let it turn your life upside down. Take a lesson from Penny. Don't let bad situations keep you from following your dreams.

Bad situations make me even more determined to reach my goals.

November 24

I'm just a hard worker who loves what he does and is blessed enough to do it every day.
—Usher

Is everybody always asking you what you want to do when you finish high school? Are people sweating you about what you're going to study in college? Well, you may not yet know what you want to do with your life. One thing you can do is ask yourself what you could spend your time doing even if you didn't get paid to do it. Whatever it is, it's probably something you'd love to do. It's also probably something you'd do well. Once you think of something you love so much you could do it for free, figure out how you can do it and get paid! Don't say, "No one would ever pay me for doing that." Don't say, "I could never pull that off." If you really want a fulfilling career or a job you love instead of one you hate, you'll do everything you can to create the job or career that will make you happy.

I do those things I'm good at and those things that make me happy.

November 25

I don't think you achieve anything in life without being disciplined.

—Lisa Leslie

If you're on your high school basketball, football, soccer, softball, baseball, wrestling, volleyball, tennis, swimming, diving, track, fencing, lacrosse, field hockey, crew or cross-country team, you know how good you feel when you win the game, match or meet. But you'll never win unless you discipline yourself and prepare for your wins. How do you discipline yourself? By working your butt off even when you don't feel like it! And you work your butt off in practice! That's what practice is for. Practice shows you and your team your strengths and weaknesses. You then use that knowledge to map out your strategy for beating your opponents. If you don't practice hard, you may be ready to play on game day, but you won't be ready to win.

I practice hard, I'm disciplined and ready to win!

November 26

At my school, I was the timekeeper. It was my responsibility to make sure the other students were on time. So it was important that I arrived always first.
—Ibrahim Hussein

As a boy growing up in Kenya during the 1960s, Ibrahim Hussein ran several miles to school, and he tried his best to always arrive first. As an adult world-class marathoner, Hussein came in first once in the New York City Marathon and three times in the Boston Marathon. As a student, Hussein was given a special responsibility. If you're a captain or co-captain of your high school sports team, you've also been given a special responsibility. You've been chosen to lead your team by example. You've been chosen to act in a way you want your teammates to emulate or imitate. You set the standards for your teammates to follow. If your standards are low, you can't really expect anyone else's to be high. So set high standards for yourself and watch your teammates follow your lead.

When I lead, I set good examples for others to follow.

November 27

I loved track, but at the time, it was a way to get to a better college. I wasn't as concerned with track as with education.

—Michael Johnson

Michael Johnson was a good high school athlete, an outstanding collegiate athlete and he is one of the baddest Olympic track stars ever! But he was also a good junior high- and high-school student who graduated from college with a degree in business. Word! If you're a good athlete, you also need to become an *educated,* good athlete. Good athletes who can't read or write or do math are headed for trouble. Why? Because really good athletes who make it to the pros use sports agents. And when you can't read or write or do math, you set yourself up to be taken advantage of. Ripped off! It's okay to dream of being a pro athlete. It's not okay to neglect your education just because you think you're headed for superstardom. If you make it to the pros, your career won't last forever. What then? No matter who you are, you need a solid education.

I understand that athletics alone won't get me through this life.

November 28

Everything has worked out for me really well. It was hard in the beginning, but now I understand why it took so long—you have to get stuff right before you get where you wanna be.
—Brandy

If you're working on something big and are tired of waiting for your break to come, chill out and listen up. Even though you may have done all the right things, sacrificed a lot of your time and put all your good energy into making your project work, you're still not in control. Who's in control? Your higher power! Your higher power is working with you to bring about your highest good. When the time is right for what you've been working on to happen for you, it will happen. I know you want it to happen now. I know you think you deserve your payoff now. But the power that created everything has everything under control—*for real!* Like Brandy says, you have to get stuff right before you get where you want to be. And your higher power knows when it's right a lot better than you do!

I trust that when the time is right, the things that I want to happen will happen.

November 29

We must be willing to go inward more often. Every strong lesson I have learned has been a feeling, intuitive one. The more I have turned inward, the more answers I have received.
　　　　　　　　　—Gloria Estefan

When you're faced with a problem what do you do? Run away or face up to it? Oftentimes, you seek advice or counseling from others when you want to face up to your problems. You also seek advice when you have a decision to make. It's good to seek advice. But it's also good to look to the spirit that lives inside you for answers. That spirit, that power, is extremely smart. That power, that spirit, is your higher power, also known as your higher intelligence, and it will speak to you and guide you if you let it. To understand how your spirit speaks to you, you have to be in touch with your spirit. One way to get in touch with your spirit is by meditating regularly. When you're in touch with your spirit you begin to trust your spirit. When you trust your spirit, you're trusting you! It's okay to ask others for advice. It's also good to look inside yourself for the answers.

The spirit within me knows the answer to any problem I face.

November 30

Ain't no gangsters living in paradise. So wake up and get something new in your life.
— Coolio

Even though violent crime overall declined during the first half of the 1990s, violent crimes by juveniles increased. But like Coolio says, a life of violence and a life of crime is not paradise. Paradise is a state of bliss, happiness or delight. But how happy are you when you have to watch your back all the time? When you can't sleep at night? When you have to front because deep down inside, you're the one who's afraid? Paradise, or happiness, can never come from outside yourself. You can't hire someone to create a paradise for you. Oh sure, you can run with people who say they'll hook you up. But the things they're hooking you up with don't bring about lasting happiness or paradise. Kids who get involved in gangs, dealing drugs and committing violent crimes not only don't live in paradise, many of them don't live very long.

My happiness comes from inside me, not from gangs, drugs or violence.

December 1

Like so many of us, let's say I come from a dysfunctional background. I've had to survive many painful situations.
—Allen Payne

Even though many kids grow up loved, appreciated and happy, unfortunately, many kids can relate to what Allen is saying. If you come from a messed up home, you're not alone. If your parents are having problems or if you don't think they care about you, it's natural for you to resent them. It's also natural for you to be ashamed of your family or lie to your friends about how things are in your family. You may even feel guilty for sometimes hating your parents or wishing you belonged to another family. But it is possible to rise above a dysfunctional family. How? By deciding that your life will be different from your parents' lives. Decide to have a better life than they do, but don't also decide to hate them for the lives they have. Forgive them for being screwed up. Allen survived a dysfunctional background. It may not be easy, but you can survive too.

I forgive my parents so that I can move on and live a happy, successful life.

December 2

If you're a child who's witnessed violence—father against mother, mother's boyfriend against her—or if you have been a victim of it, you've got some special issues that have to be addressed—your fear, your anger, your pain.

—Dr. Deborah Prothrow-Stith

Fear, anger and pain. Those are feelings we all know all too well. If you're a kid who's been beaten by your parents, you probably have even more fear, anger and pain than kids who haven't been beaten. If your parents are beating you with their fists, if they're slapping you around, if they're beating you with belts, coat hangers or any objects, they're abusing you and it has to stop. You may think they're beating you because "all Puerto Rican parents are strict on their kids," or because "that's just the way my dad is." No matter what you may think or how much you love your parents, if they're beating you, it's not right and it has to stop. Get help from a counselor if you're being abused by your parents or by anyone else.

I am doing what it takes to heal from the painful things I've experienced.

December 3

When my foster parents or people told me I couldn't accomplish anything, I wouldn't say 'Well, I'm going to try and do it anyway.' It was more like, 'I can't believe they said I can't do it.'
—Antwone Fisher

If you're in foster care, and the people taking care of you aren't loving you, respecting you and believing in you, listen up: You are a great kid! Being in foster care doesn't mean there's something wrong with you, it just means there were some problems at home that needed taking care of, and you needed a different environment to live in. If your foster parents or others are telling you what you can't do, be just as *incredulous* as Antwone! When you're incredulous about something someone says, you can't believe they said what they said! Those people don't know what you're made of. They don't know how strong you are inside. The good news is that you know how special you are! You know you can do anything you put your mind to! You know!

People who doubt that I'm going to make it in life are in for the shock of their lives!

December 4

It's a tradition in the Hispanic culture to try to go along with your family. I was a business major because that's what my family is into, but I got to a point where I was not happy.
—Bill Cuevas

Different cultures have different traditions. Sometimes, the traditions handed down through the generations of your family seem old fashioned, corny or unfair. It's not easy when you want one thing for yourself and your family or your parents want something different. But just because your parents want something for you you don't want for yourself, doesn't mean they don't love you and want you to be happy. Parents often want for you what they think is best. By the time you graduate from high school or enter college, it's time to begin making more of your own decisions about what will make you happy. If you and your family disagree about what you should be doing, that's okay. What's not okay is for you to do things as a young adult that make you unhappy just to please your parents.

I am responsible for my happiness.

December 5

I know where I am, and I know where I want to go.
It's just a matter of staying focused.
—Janet Jackson

Making your dreams come true requires a lot of hard
work. Believing in yourself is great, but there's
something called being focused that is just as
important. To focus on something means to
concentrate all your attention and effort on it. So
when you're focused on your goals, you become a
slave to them. When you're focused on your goals,
you give your goals your undivided attention. You
also give your goals your maximum effort. You do
this in the classroom, on the track field, on the
basketball court—wherever. Many things will come
along to try to cause you to lose focus—to lose sight
of your goals. Ignore those things. Push them aside.
Having dreams and goals is great. But your dreams
won't come true, and you'll never reach your goals
unless you stay focused.

I stay focused on my goal.

December 6

Either you tryin' to work, you tryin' to go to school, or you standin' on that corner.
—J. Quest

A job. School. The streets. What's it going to be for you? What do you want? If you want a job, you've got to have some basic skills and some basic knowledge if you expect to get hired. Those skills and that knowledge are obtained in school. If you're planning on going to college, you've got to have decent grades. You also have to have accomplished things, both in school and outside of school, to make college administrators think you'd be a good addition to their school. Now, if you standing on that corner you don't have to meet very many requirements at all.

I am preparing for my tomorrow by the things I do today.

December 7

The reason I'm hard on people is because I know how much it's going to take for them to get to the point where I'm at. I don't want to be only one with a car and money.

—Sean "Puffy" Combs

Your parents, teachers and coaches are oftentimes hard on you for a good reason. They want you to succeed! What's difficult for you to understand when you're young is that parents, teachers and coaches have already been where you are. Your parents faced peer pressure when they were growing up, too. Maybe it wasn't as tough as the pressures that challenge you, but they know what peer pressure is. Your coaches wanted to be star players too, and sometimes were, when they were in school. And believe it or not, your teachers weren't always teachers. So don't be so quick to dis your parents, your coaches and your teachers when they try to give you advice. *No, they don't know everything. But neither do you.* And believe it or not, in many cases, they've been through what you're going through.

I listen to those who are older and wiser than me when they're trying to help me.

December 8

We all have to remember that we do have power and responsibility.

—Farai Chideya

Sometimes, you feel like you don't have any power. You feel as if your parents or your teachers have power over you. Well, parents and teachers do exercise control over you to help you grow and develop into a mature adult. But you do have power, lots of power, inside you. You have the same power inside you that created the Universe, and you have the power of choice. You can choose to obey your parents and heed your teacher's advice, or you can choose not to. You can choose to go along with the crowd or you can choose not to. You can choose to continue complaining when things go wrong or you can choose to make some changes. See, you really do have power! And because you're not the only person alive, you also have responsibility. Your responsibility is to use your power wisely so your choices don't cause anyone else pain or unhappiness.

The power that created the Universe is the same power inside me, and I use it wisely.

December 9

I came to the realization that I can't please everyone,
but I can give 110 percent.
—Montell Jordan

You can never satisfy everyone. The things you do
that make one friend happy could very well make
another friend mad. So then what do you do?
Montell has some good thoughts. You give
everything you have, and then some, to try to do
what's right. If you're doing what's right, right for you
and right by others, then you shouldn't stress whether
or not everybody likes you or what you're doing. You
weren't put on this earth to please everybody. You
weren't put on this earth to make everybody like you.
You weren't put on this earth to make everybody
happy. You were put on this earth to fulfill your life's
mission and to be a good citizen of the world. Being
a good citizen doesn't mean everybody has to like
you. Being a good citizen doesn't mean you
constantly put yourself out to do what others want.

*I understand that it's okay if the whole world doesn't
like everything I do.*

December 10

You have to control and master anger.
　　　　　—Chico DeBarge

Getting angry is normal. But getting angry can be scary because you sometimes feel angry enough to really hurt someone. Often, you're angry at those closest to you—parents, brothers and sisters, friends. And it seems weird but sometimes, you can feel much love and much hate for people all in the same day. So how do you control anger? Whenever you feel anger, take several slow, deep breaths. Then, keep breathing and really listen to the sound of yourself breathing. Concentrate! As you concentrate, close your eyes. You're beginning to feel yourself calm down. If your hand is balled up into a fist, unball your fist. Now, as you're still breathing, relax the muscles in your face. Unclench your jaw. Relax the muscles in your neck and back. As you're still breathing and concentrating on your breath, relax your face further by breaking out into a smile!

I automatically calm myself down when I become angry.

December 11

I don't like people who say "no, no Erykah." I don't like nobody trying to kill your ideas 'cause they doubt themselves. That's tired to me.
—Erykah Badu

Erykah's right. People who doubt themselves will bring their doubts and their negativity to you! But why are some people negative and why do some people doubt themselves? Negative ideas become a part of you, a part of your unconscious mind when you hear them over and over and over. The way to fight against all those negative things you hear, is to replace them with something positive. The minute you hear something negative about yourself or about life, say something positive over and over and over about yourself or about life. Just think what would have happened if Erykah had listened to the negative people she came across. We wouldn't have songs like "On and On" and "Tyrone" to jam to!

When a negative thought pops into my head, I replace it with a positive thought!

December 12

We were all expected to do well at everything.
—Jessye Norman

Some of your parents, grandparents and other relatives have achieved great things, and they expect that you'll achieve great things, too. If success runs in your family, you probably want to continue the tradition. Sometimes, though, the decision to achieve great things and live up to family traditions makes you afraid—afraid you won't be as successful as your parents or relatives and afraid you'll let them down. It's normal to have a little anxiety when trying to live up to high expectations. But when you don't want to do what others expect of you, you feel pressure, and you have more than a little anxiety. Just remember, you'll be a lot happier in life if you go after the things you know will make you happy instead of doing something because you think it's expected of you.

I am successful when I follow my heart and do things that bring me happiness.

December 13

Anyone interested in arts as a career should push towards fulfilling their education first.
—Adrienne-Joi Johnson

It's okay, in fact it's great, if you want to be an actor or a singer or a dancer or an artist or a playwright when you grow up. But like Adrienne says, if you want a career in the arts, you still need to be educated. Actors aren't always acting, and when they're between jobs, they have to have enough education to be able to support themselves. The same is true for dancers, singers, artists and playwrights. And once you make it big in your chosen profession, how will you protect your interests, your money if you haven't gained sufficient knowledge in economics, language arts, and history? If you know anything about history, you know many great artists have been ripped off by people who took advantage of their limited knowledge. If you want a career in the arts, you need to be an educated, informed artist!

My education comes first.

December 14

Ignore those who would tell you how to make the quick dollar or take the quick fix.
—Percy Sutton

Fast money can often lead to slow time—you know like eight to 10 months in juvenile jail. Kids who make fast money by selling drugs or stealing cars or burglarizing homes often aren't considering the consequences of their actions. Once you're caught, convicted and sentenced for your illegal, high-paying job, you'll be spending time in lock up where you'll work for free! In the big house, or adult prison, prisoners who may have once made $400 a day illegally, have to accept making 50 cents an hour. When you look honestly and seriously at the consequences of fast, illegal money, that legal, minimum wage job may not look so bad.

I understand the value of making an honest dollar.

December 15

I really believe that a man and a woman together raising a family, is the purest form of happiness we can experience.
—Will Smith

Have you heard politicians talk about "family values" on TV? Well, there's no need to let politicians tell you what family values are. You're smart enough and mature enough to know how valuable good families are to society. You know that everybody needs a family to love, appreciate and care for them. You also know that raising a family is not easy. You know that your parents have one of the toughest jobs on earth! If you're planning on having a family later on, cool! Take care of business now so that when the time comes for you to start your own family, you'll be ready. If you've already started your family, I hope you're doing everything you can to make your family a strong one.

I understand the value of a good family.

December 16

I mean, when I was coming up, being called a bitch was fighting words. And now it's so common. It bothers me.

—Queen Latifah

On October 16, 1995, between 800,000 and *one million* black men gathered on the mall in Washington D.C. for the historic Million Man March. The march challenged many men to pay more attention to their spirit within and to understand what it *really* means to be a man. Many of the men who congregated took a pledge to "never use the "B" word to describe any female, but particularly my own black sister." Some women who heard the men take the pledge decided that they too would stop calling other women bitches. Maybe it's time you stepped up and figured out what it *really* means to be a man. Whether you're a young man or a young woman, maybe it's time you took the pledge to eliminate the "B" word from your conversation if you haven't already.

I talk to people the way I want them to talk to me.

December 17

If someone raises his hand to hit you, I don't care how fine he is, you let that thang go!
—Yolanda Adams

If you're with a guy who hits you and he's been hitting you for a while, you may start believing you deserve to be hit. Once you believe that, you've given up that part of yourself which felt special and unique. You may stay with him because you think he'll be devastated if you leave him, and you don't want him to hurt. You may stay with him because you love him and have thoughts of marrying him. Well, very few teens marry their first love or high school boyfriend. Like Yolanda says, as hard as it may be, if he hits you, let him go! You're not responsible for his hurt and his pain if you leave him. You're responsible for you and it's your responsibility to deal with your own hurt and pain. Remember, you can only change you! Start believing you deserve a good relationship then get out of the abusive relationship before you end up in the hospital or dead!

I have a healthy, loving relationship without physical or emotional abuse.

December 18

What goes around comes back around ten times worse.

—Donald Faison

There's no getting around it—what you put out, you get back. Everything you do in life has consequences. You may not want to believe it, but you're in control of what happens to you. Your thoughts and actions determine how your life will be. Why? Because that's how the Universe set it up. That way, people have a reason to do good things and think good thoughts. They also have a reason to not do bad things and think bad thoughts. Remember, your thoughts lead to your actions. And your actions determine what happens to you. So, if you want to get love, give love. If you want peace in your life, don't bring stress and confusion into someone else's life. If you want good to come into your life, make sure you're not the one bringing bad to someone else's life.

I treat others right and I do good things because I want to be treated right and I want good things to come to me.

December 19

Parents, take care of your babies! If mothers and fathers would take time out and create a relationship with their children now, they won't have to rehabilitate later.

—John P. Kee

You probably realize how important it is to have your parents there for you. If you're a teenage parent, then you've got to realize how important it is for you to be there for your child. Ladies, don't drop out of school because you're pregnant! You need to be educated to make it in this world. You need to be able to teach your baby how to make it in this world. Boys, don't run out on your child. Your baby needs you! Your baby needs you the same way you need your father! Your baby needs food and clothes, but it also needs your love. It needs its mothers love. Your baby is depending on both of you to nurture it and to teach it right from wrong. It's a big responsibility, but if you don't take responsibility for your kid, who will?

I am a responsible teenage parent.

December 20

While I appreciate beauty, I've learned that love is not just a sexual thing.
—Leon

Some teens' responses when asked to say the first thing that comes to mind when they hear the word *love*: Warm. Good. Relationship. Wonderful. Safe. Being there for somebody. Caring. Kind. Makes you feel good about yourself. High self-esteem. Feels good. Unconditional. Deep. Mom. Truth. Pain. Commitment. Trust. Attention. Friends. Husband. Sex. Faithful. Honesty. Kids. Important. Girls. Faithfulness. Special. Trusting. Marriage. Agape. Parents. Hurtful. Danger. Hate. People.

Love is the power that lives inside me and the force that holds the Universe together.

December 21

If we think we need to get something from another, we will love that person when we get what we think we want, and we will hate that person when we do not.

—Jerry Jamplosky

You're setting yourself up for disappointment when you expect others to satisfy your needs for love. Sure others can love you. And yes, your parents and your caregivers are your first source of love when you're a child. But as you mature, you'll understand that the love you want from others has to first come from you! Sound wack? Well, it's not. If you don't know how to love yourself, you won't be able to give love to others. And if you don't know how to give love, you won't be able to receive love. It's perfectly normal to want to be loved by your boyfriend or girlfriend. But if you're dependent on their love and you don't have self love, what happens to you when they pack up their love and take it away?

I am learning to give and receive love.

December 22

But after you get caught up in that whole sleeping around thing, as you grow older and wiser, you realize that you need something more. You realize that mental bond is more important than the physical act of sex.

—Gerald Levert

When you're a teenager, you may think having sex is the thing to do. But as Gerald says, as you grow older and wiser, you realize what sex is and what it isn't. Sex is not a toy, even though many, many people, adults as well as teenagers act as though it is. Having sex is natural, and it plays a natural, healthy role in a relationship. But sex is just one part of being in a relationship. For most people, sleeping around doesn't give them what they're really searching for—*love.* You won't find love by having sex with someone. And even though you might think having sex is the greatest thing going, believe me, there are things that are much greater.

The older I get, the smarter I get!

December 23

I'm not just going to give my body to anybody...It's too precious.

—Nia Long

Some teens responses when asked to say the first thing that comes to mind when they hear the word *sex:* All that! Good! Love. Beautiful. Caring and sharing. Bond between two people, but not love. Resentment. Regret. Children. Diseases. Condoms. Female. Disappointment. Male. Intimacy. Safety. Pregnancy. Protection. Enjoyable. Uncaring. Pretty Woman. Marriage. Abstinent. Boys. Babies. Bed.

I am a spiritual being living in a physical body, and I treat my body and my spirit like they're something precious.

December 24

I get angry when I hear racist remarks. But they will not poison me.

—Regina Taylor

I get angry when I hear racist remarks, *but they will not poison me!* They will not make me hate. I will not use racist remarks and racist people as a reason to hate. I will never give anyone else power over my actions and my emotions. Why? Because I am in control of me. And I'm secure enough to know that a person who makes racists remarks is ignorant and needs help and healing. I get angry when I hear racist remarks, but I turn my anger into activism. I am active in the fight against racism and white superiority and discrimination. I will never allow racism to keep me from achieving what I want to achieve in life. I will never use America's racism as an excuse to give up. I know racism exists, and I know racist people exist, but they will not poison me.

Racism has no power over me.

December 25

Profit, gain and the extraordinary materialism of our society are weakening the human condition.
—Octavio Paz

When Octavio talks about the human condition, he's talking about us. He's talking about the world we live in. He's talking about how we need to treat each other in order to survive and in order for our planet to survive. When we don't love our planet and everything in it, we weaken our planet and everything in it. If we continue to destroy our planet earth with pollution, we can't go to another planet and buy clean rivers, lakes and oceans. We can't go shopping in the Universe for new rain forests. And when we don't love each other, we also weaken the human condition. When you understand what love is, you'll realize it can't be bought or sold or traded. Love is a gift! But giving someone a present or some money doesn't prove your love to them. If we don't treat each other in a loving way, all the Christmas presents and all the money in the world won't make up for it.

I demonstrate my love for others and for the planet I live on 365 days a year.

December 26

I knew that I would have a better life than the one I lived as a child.

—Rosie O'Donnell

Rosie O'Donnell does have a better life than the one she lived as a child. When Rosie was ten, her mother died of breast cancer. Rosie's father had a hard time dealing with his wife's death so Rosie took on a lot of responsibility for her brothers and sisters at a young age. Rosie also had a hard time accepting her mom's death. For a long time afterward, when someone would call and ask to speak to her mother, she'd lie and say her mom was in the shower. If you're having a rough time right now, I know you wish the rough times would end. I know you wish things were different. Well, right now, things are what they are, but as Rosie says, things do get better! Why not do what Rosie did when she was kid and believe that you will have a better life? Sure things can get worse. But things can also get better! Decide what you want, better or worse, and make it happen!

Each day I'm alive, my life is getting better and better.

December 27

A main part of life is doing what *you* have to do and then going on down the road.
—Willie Banks Jr.

There's a time to chill and a time to get busy. There's a time to play around and a time to be serious. Every hour of every day, you decide what time it is for you. Sometimes, you make wise choices. Others times, your choices aren't so smart. But like Willie Banks Jr. says—you do what you have to do then you go on down the road. If you do what you have to do, and you do it right, you can leave and never look back. Sometimes, though, you have to do things twice or three times before you get it right. That's okay. You won't do everything the right way the first time you try. What's important is that you keep trying. Once you accomplish what you set out to accomplish, take a look back, smile and feel good about what you've done. Go on down the road!

I keep trying until I get it right.

December 28

I mean, I was a teenager. My mother was hard on me and I couldn't understand why until now. I didn't understand there was a reason for it.
—Mary J. Blige

There is a reason why your parents are hard on you. And, like Mary, you may not understand the reason until you're older. Even if someone told you now why your parents are so hard on you, you may hear what they say, but still not understand or accept what they say. That's normal and that's okay. But remember, there have been many, many kids who have grown up, looked back on how hard and strict their parents were and gone up to their parents and thanked them for being so hard and so strict. There have also been many kids who didn't have strict parents who grew up, looked back and wished their parents had been more strict!

I may not understand everything now, but as I mature, I understand a lot more.

December 29

The solutions ultimately have to come from the young people themselves. We are the future, and we make of our future what we make of it.
—Chelsea Clinton

Your future is on you! And everything you think and do today affects what will happen to you tomorrow. But don't let that scare you. Learn not to fear the future. How? First, learn to be at peace right now. Chill. Have faith. Have faith in yourself, and have faith in your higher power. Second, believe you can create the kind of future you want for yourself and your world. Third, do whatever you have to do now to create the kind of future you believe you can have. If that means getting better grades, get better grades. If that means staying out of trouble, stay out of trouble. If that means you stop judging people by their skin color, then stop! Believe that you can help change society. And don't say, "that's easier said than done." Everything is! Be positive, and be willing to work. It's your future, and like Chelsea says, you make of it what you make of it!

My future is in my hands.

December 30

If you combine body, mind and spirit, there's nothing you can't do.

—Shawne Byrant, M.D.

You are body, mind and *spirit!* And your body, mind and spirit will work together to give you all the things you want in life—if you allow them to! Too many people underestimate the power the mind and spirit have over the body. Too many also neglect the spirit all together. Remember, life is not just about money or material things! Life is also not just about being smart and getting good grades. You are body, mind and spirit so take time to connect with your spirit by meditating or praying or worshipping. Allow your spirit to work with your mind and your body. When you're in touch with your spirit you know nothing is impossible. And when you stay connected with your spirit, you're better able to handle life's stressful situations, and your body is less likely to become sick or filled with disease.

My body, mind and spirit work together to bring me peace, happiness and good health!

December 31

The majority of today's youth have a 'don't give a fuck' attitude. That's what's going on in NY all the way to Cali and in between.
—Kool G Rap

Don't be part of Kool G Rap's majority. Prove him wrong!

I am valuable bean and my life matters!
I am a gift from God... to the world!
I am intelligent and I have stuff I can work!
I have a mission in life, and I will discover what it is!
I am in control of my future!
I am body, mind and spirit.
I know where I come from and I'm proud of it!
I am beautiful just like I am!
I have inside me everything I need to be successful!
As I mature, I learn more and more about me!
Racism has no power over me!
I believe in myself! I am a good person!
Yes I Can!

I love and approve of myself.

Congratulations and Happy New Year!

Peace Out

INDEX

Anger Management 1/22, 2/15, 2/16, 2/21, 3/17, 3/24, 7/22, 12/11
Anthony, Marc 8/12
Ashanti Proverb 9/11

Babyface 3/1, 8/29,
Badu, Erykah 12/11
Baker, Anita 4/25
Baldwin, James 5/1
Banks Jr., Willie 12/27
Baraka, Ras 7/10
Barkley, Charles 1/14
Being bi- or multi-racial 8/1, 8/2, 8/5
Beltran, Michelle 9/12
Benitez, Jellybean 6/4
Berry, Halle 9/27
Big Lez 8/31
Black Panther Party 7/20
Blades, Ruben 2/21
Blank, Kenny 4/29
Blige, Mary J. 1/17, 12/28
Bogues, Muggsy 8/20
Boricua College 5/25
Breaking up with your girl or your guy 9/30, 12/17
Brandy 4/15, 11/28

Nas 4/16
National Domestic Violence Hotline Number
10/25
National Hispanic University 5/25
Native Americans 6/28
Neilson, Rex 8/14
Nieves, Anna Maria 9/15
"Nigger" 7/13
Norman, Jessye 12/12
Novello, Antonia 8/23

O'Donnell, Rosie 12/26
Olajuwon, Hakeem 5/12
Olmos, Edward James 5/2
O'Neal, Shaquille 9/24
O'Neil, Buck 8/9

Padilla, Alejandro "Alex" 7/29
Parents 1/13, 1/14, 1/18, 1/19, 4/15, 7/28, 8/22,
9/16, 9/23, 10/27, 10/28, 12/1, 12/2, 12/4, 12/7,
12/12, 12/29
Payne, Allen 12/1
Paz, Octavio 12/25
Peer Pressure 1/4, 1/5, 2/24, 3/12, 3/22, 6/15,
7/29, 9/1, 11/10, 11/16, 11/22

Tyson, Mike 8/16

Unconscious Thoughts 3/6, 4/27, 12/11
Usher 11/24

Van Peebles, Melvin 3/29
Vedder, Eddie of Pearl Jam 6/14
Velazquez, Nydia 7/21
Velez, Lauren 6/19
Violence 2/16, 2/21, 6/30, 7/1, 7/3, 11/16, 11/30
Voices of the Homeless 8/14

Walker, Madame C.J. 8/18
Warning from someone who's not having it!
4/20
Washington, Denzel 3/28
Waters, Maxine 11/8
Wayans, Keenen Ivory 3/21
Wayans, Marlon 8/22
Wells-Barnett, Ida B. 5/26
Whitaker, Forest 3/25
White Superiority 5/9, 12/24
Williams, Bob 5/28
Williams, Montel 2/5
Williams, Venus 8/28

To order copies of *It's All Good!*

**Send $14.95* per book,
plus shipping and handling to:**

Emp! Emp! Press
P.O. Box 21222
Washington, D.C. 20009-1222

Shipping and Handling

1-2 books	**$3.00**
3-5 books	**$5.00**
6-10 books	**$7.00**

Remember to include your <u>name and mailing address</u> and please allow two to three weeks for delivery.

*Washington D.C. residents add a 5.75% sales tax